3D Printed Science Projects

Ideas for Your Classroom, Science Fair, or Home

Joan Horvath
Rich Cameron

Apress®

3D Printed Science Projects: Ideas for Your Classroom, Science Fair, or Home

ISBN-13 (pbk): 978-1-4842-1324-7

ISBN-13 (electronic): 978-1-4842-1323-0

Managing Director: Welmoed Spahr
Lead Editor: Michelle Lowman
Editorial Board: Steve Anglin, Pramila Balan, Louise Corrigan, Jonathan Gennick,
    Robert Hutchinson, Celestin Suresh John, Michelle Lowman, James Markham,
    Susan McDermott, Matthew Moodie, Jeffrey Pepper, Douglas Pundick,
    Ben Renow-Clarke, Gwenan Spearing
Coordinating Editor: Mark Powers
Copy Editor: Corbin Collins
Compositor: SPi Global
Indexer: SPi Global
Artist: SPi Global

In memory of Zillabell "Jane" Friesen

Contents at a Glance

Contents

About the Authors

Joan Horvath and **Rich Cameron** are the cofounders of Nonscriptum LLC based in Pasadena, California. Nonscriptum consults for educational and scientific users in the areas of 3D printing and maker technologies. Joan and Rich are particularly interested in finding ways to use makertech to make scientific research cheaper and more accessible to the public.

This book is their latest collaboration, following their earlier works *Mastering 3D Printing* (Apress, 2014), *The New Shop Class: Getting Started with 3D Printing, Arduino, and Wearable Tech* (Apress, 2015), and *3D Printing with MatterControl* (Apress, 2015). They also teach online classes in 3D printing and makertech for LERN Network's U Got Class continuing education program. Links for all of the above are on their website, www.nonscriptum.com.

In addition to her work with Rich, Joan also has an appointment as Core Adjunct faculty for National University's College of Letters and Sciences. She has taught at the university level in a variety of institutions, both in Southern California and online. Before she and Rich started Nonscriptum, she held a variety of entrepreneurial positions, including Vice President of Business Development at a Kickstarter-funded 3D-printer company. Joan started her career with 16 years at the NASA/Caltech Jet Propulsion Laboratory, where she worked in programs including the technology transfer office, the Magellan spacecraft to Venus, and the TOPEX/Poseidon oceanography spacecraft. She holds an undergraduate degree from MIT in Aeronautics and Astronautics and a master's degree in Engineering from UCLA.

Rich (known online as "Whosawhatsis") is an experienced open source developer who has been a key member of the RepRap 3D-printer development community for many years. His designs include the original spring/lever extruder mechanism used on many 3D printers, the RepRap Wallace, and the Deezmaker Bukito portable 3D printer. By building and modifying several of the early open source 3D printers to wrestle unprecedented performance out of them, he has become an expert at maximizing the print quality of filament-based printers. When he's not busy making every aspect of his own 3D printers better, from slicing software to firmware and hardware, he likes to share that knowledge and experience online so that he can help make everyone else's printers better too.

Acknowledgments

The consumer 3D-printing ecosystem would not exist in its current form without the open source 3D-printing hardware and software community, and in particular Marius Kintel, the main developer and maintainer of OpenSCAD software, and his collaborators for their software, which was used to develop the objects in this book. We are also grateful for the support of the MatterHackers team and their MatterControl software, particular Lars Brubaker, Kevin Pope, and Mara Hitner for their support during the writing of this book. The maker community as a whole has also been very supportive. The picture of Joan and Rich in the "About the Authors" section was taken at the 2015 San Mateo Makerfaire by Ethan Etnyre; we appreciate all the inspiration we have gotten by looking at projects made by everyone at maker events large and small.

The Apress production team made this process seamless for the most part, and was there with virtual needle and thread for the occasions where it was not. We dealt most directly with Mark Powers, Michelle Lowman, James Markham, Corbin Collins and Welmoed Spahr, but we also appreciate the many we did not see.

We picked a lot of scientists' brains as we thought about how to model some of the concepts in this book. We particularly thank high school teacher Michael Cheverie for his insights into teaching chemistry. Joan's longsuffering astronomer husband, Stephen Unwin, was a huge help as we went back into some basic physics or just tried to get past the 3D modeling equivalent of writer's block. Frank Carsey, Dan Berry, Tim Thibault, and many others helped us out by reading a chapter draft or helping us think through alternative ways that we might model something.

We thank the staff, teachers, and students of the Windward School in Los Angeles for inspiration and discussions of how students learn, particularly Cynthia Beals, James Bologna, Lyn Hoge, Simon Huss, Dorothy Lee, Geraldine Loveless, Kevin Kloeker, Ernie Levoney, Tri Nguyen, Karalyn Raymon, Colin Rose, and Regina Rubio. We also were inspired to create these models in part by discussions with people in the community of teachers of the visually impaired, notably Mike Cheverie, Lore Schindler, Yue-Ting Siu, and the participants in the Benetech workshop organized by Lisa Wadors.

Finally, we are grateful to our families for putting up with our endless brainstorming, kitchen table commandeering, and test runs of explanations. This book has been a long pull for everyone, but we think it will be well worth the wait.

Introduction

When we started our 3D-printing and makertech consulting company, we joked that we were going to call it "Now What?" because that was what schools seemed to say after they bought a 3D printer. We hope that this book takes a step toward answering that question.

We saw that students, parents, and teachers would be excited about using a 3D printer, might download a 3D model, print it, and then wonder what to do next. Or, they might get into creating models from scratch, and get discouraged by the limitations of easier 3D-modeling programs or the learning curves of the more capable ones.

In this book, we try to create a middle path: models that you could just print, but that would be reasonably easy to alter if you wanted to do more. Further, we designed the models so that they would be useful for learning science or math principles while you were changing their features. In particular we wanted to create some seeds of science fair or extra-credit projects—that is, open-ended, meaty explorations that could be explored at a variety of levels.

We were surprised at how hard this turned out to be. Most textbooks and online sites endlessly recycle versions of the same 2D projection of models of science concepts. In each chapter, we have a "Learning Like a Maker" section where we talk about our adventures in defining and implementing the models—which in some cases involved finding online copies of 1935 manuscripts (signed off by a Wright brother and Charles Lindbergh!) and in others meant figuring out what to do after a scientific experts who implied that everyone teaches the subject at hand the way it is drawn in textbooks, but you unlearn all that in grad school to get to the *real* way.

This book presumes that you know a little bit about 3D printing already. If not, Appendix A and the resources linked there should get you up to speed. The models are all written using the OpenSCAD free and open source 3D-modeling program. If you know how to program in a language like C, Java, or Python, that will help, but it's not strictly necessary to alter the models. Appendix A and the OpenSCAD materials linked there will help you out with that too.

We have found that teachers use 3D printers in one of two fundamental ways. Either they want to create a model to pass around in class to help students visualize a concept, or they want students to use a printer either to learn engineering and design per se or to cement physical concepts like levers and gears. Since most of these models would lend themselves to being used either way, we have not included a grade level or explicit lesson plans.

To show our readers who are teachers (in the United States) what we had in mind, though, at the end of most chapters we suggest Next Generation Science Standards that we thought might benefit from these models. These science standards, from the group NGSS Lead States, are documented in *Next Generation Science Standards: For States, By States* (The National Academies Press, 2013). Links are given at the end of relevant chapters. If you are a teacher, you may want to check with your state or school standards as well to see the best fit.

The models span a variety of topics, and we tried to cover as many disciplines as possible. Briefly, here is what you can look forward to:

> Chapter 1 gives you a few options to print many different types of mathematical surface. This ability underlies some of the other models.
>
> Chapter 2 creates models of waves to allow you to explore what happens when various waves overlap and interact. You can print yourself a model of Young's famous double-slit experiment to see how light from two slits can interfere.
>
> Chapter 3 takes us back to Newton and Kepler to learn about planets and stars and how they speed up and slow down in their orbits.
>
> Chapter 4 allows you to create wings with classic airfoil shapes from the early days of flight. You will be able to make yourself a very simplistic test stand that you can use to measure the lift from the wing with just a fan and a postal scale.
>
> Chapter 5 lets you create basic models of all the "simple machines"—wedge, inclined plane, lever, pulleys, and screws.
>
> Chapter 6 allows you to model plants and their ecosystems, and to design plants for different environments. Maybe you can create a garden for another planet (or for Earth after another few hundred years of climate change).
>
> Chapter 7 lets you begin to explore carbon atoms, and how water molecules come together to make two different types of ice crystals.
>
> Chapter 8 explores 2D and 3D trusses and how you can use them in various explorations.
>
> As we noted earlier, Appendix A reviews how to 3D print, and Appendix B aggregates all the links in the book.

Finally, we are making the 3D-printable models used in this book (although not the book itself!) open source, licensed under a Creative Commons Attribution-NonCommerical-ShareAlike 4.0 International License (https://creativecommons.org/licenses/by-nc-sa/4.0/). That means you can use them for noncommercial purposes (in a classroom, for instance) and alter and remix them as long as you credit us. Appendix A has some notes about where to find the repositories if you would like to add to these models. We hope these models are the beginning of a set of models that students everywhere can play with and learn from.

CHAPTER 1

■■■

3D Math Functions

Since so much scientific visualization starts with looking at underlying mathematics, we are beginning this book on 3D printing for science projects with a chapter on 3D printing mathematical functions. The basic models in this chapter are intended to be a starter set that you alter to 3D print whatever function you like, within the boundaries we will get to in a later section.

Math Modeling for 3D Printing

It seems like it should be easy to just put an equation into a program and have the printer "draw" it somehow, like some sort of 3D pen plotter. However, if a 3D printer head just tried to follow an equation, it would have no way of knowing how to avoid material that had already laid down, so we have to go about it in a bit more roundabout way.

3D Printing

3D printers require a several-step process from the first idea to a finished print. First, you need to develop a 3D model, as we will in this chapter. Models in this chapter (and most of the remainder of the book) are based on the free, open source 3D solid modeling program OpenSCAD (www.openscad.org). OpenSCAD allows you to encode geometrical models in a language that is sort of a subset of the C programming language. Good documentation is available by clicking the Documentation button on the OpenSCAD site's home page.

Then, other software takes this model and slices it into layers, which the printer will then create one at a time, typically from the bottom up. We will use the open source MatterControl host program throughout this book, available free from www.mattercontrol.com. Appendix A talks more about things you should know about OpenSCAD, MatterControl, and 3D printing in general.

Electronic supplementary material The online version of this chapter (doi:10.1007/978-1-4842-1323-0_1) contains supplementary material, which is available to authorized users.

■ **Tip**   This book presumes you are generally familiar with 3D printing practices. If not, you can learn how to use a printer from Joan's previous book, *Mastering 3D Printing* (Apress, 2014) or our book *3D Printing With MatterControl* (Apress, 2015). Unless we specifically note otherwise, prints in this book were created on a Deezmaker Bukito in polylactic acid (PLA) plastic, using the MatterSlice engine in MatterControl (although we could have used any software compatible with an open source printer).

Math Background

This chapter presumes you know what a *function* is—a relationship among a number of variables. In this case, we are dealing with functions using three variables, which we will call x, y, and z. Function notation looks like this: $z = f(x,y)$. All that means is that our variable, z, can be computed for any given pair of values for the x and y variables. Having three variables means we can define shapes in three dimensions, with one variable corresponding to each dimension. Normally these three-dimensional shapes would be shown on a page with two-dimensional projections. Often, this is fine and you can see what is going on. Sometimes, however, it really helps to hold a 3D model in your hand and turn it this way and that. This chapter will give you the ability to do that for many types of functions.

■ **Note**   3D printing convention holds that x and y are in the plane of the platform that your model is being built up on, and z is vertical height above that. In other words, the bottom of the surfaces generated in this chapter is always the $z = 0$ plane. In this convention, you always have to *transform* what you are printing to have z greater than or equal to zero, since you cannot build under the platform. In other words, if you know that z would be negative for some values of x and y that you want to use, you may have to add an offset to your equation so that z is always greater than zero and remember that the offset is there when you think about what your model represents.

We will get you started with a model entirely in OpenSCAD that creates surfaces of functions $z = f(x,y)$, where x and y are the plane of the 3D printer's build platform, and z is the height of the surface above that plane. First we will show you how the basic 3D math model Rich has written and included here works, and what kind of functions you can print. Then we will show you a simple model that creates surfaces that might be a starting point for your own projects in OpenSCAD.

Alternatively you may have code you developed that produces a surface you would like to 3D print. It may not be practical to port that code to an OpenSCAD model. We will also show you an example in which we wrote a separate Python script that produces a file, which is then read into OpenSCAD and made into a surface. Finally we will give you some ideas about how you might use these tools as a teacher or as part of a student project.

Others (see links at "Where To Learn More" later in this chapter) have used more sophisticated mathematics modeling programs, but our desire here is to make this completely accessible and free so that you can get started without investing in software, at least at the beginning of your explorations.

Creating Surfaces Entirely in OpenSCAD

In this section we show you how to create a polynomial with a flat base. In the next section we show you what a print of a double-sided surface looks like using the same OpenSCAD code with different parameters. This model was written to be simple and easy to alter, which means that it does not check for complicated problems, like functions that go to infinity or other mathematically bad behavior. It does, however, let you input a function $f(x,y)$ (as you can see in Listing 1-1). It uses OpenSCAD's polyhedron module to accomplish this.

Making a Smooth Surface with a Flat Bottom

Listing 1-1 is the OpenSCAD model that creates a flat-bottomed "slice" of a surface, like a chunk cut out of a mountain range. The function in this example is $z = f(x, y) = 0.01$ $(x - 50)(y - 50) + 30$, and the 3D print will go from $x = 0$ to 99 and $y = 0$ to 99. This creates a "saddle point" structure, as shown in Figure 1-1. The model will create a surface $xmax$ mm in x and $ymax$ mm in y, with z height computed in mm. If the resulting structure is too big (by default, 99 mm by 99 mm on the bottom, or a bit less than 4 inches square), then you can scale the whole piece in your 3D-printing software. Figure 1-1 was scaled down to one-quarter scale.

Figure 1-1. *Saddle function with a flat bottom. Printed at quarter scale, so each side is about 25 mm, or just under an inch long. Layer height was 0.2 mm*

3

The values of x and y go from 0 to *xmax* and *ymax* respectively. A maximum of 100 points in each dimension (*xmax* = 99 and *ymax* = 99) is allowed. The model will step in units of 1, which cannot be changed. If you want your model to step in smaller or larger increments, you will need to scale the variable in the equation.

For example, if in your original equation you had a function you wanted to increment by 0.02 in each step, replace the x in your original equation by $(0.02 * x)$ to accomplish the same thing when you increment by 1. Or if you want to step from –500 to –400 in the original function, replace the x in your original function with $(x - 500)$ everywhere to accomplish the same thing. Be careful if variables are raised to a power, or are inside a function like cosine, that you do this scaling correctly and consistently.

■ **Caution**   Because we are creating a flat bottom, the equation being represented here is actually $0 <= z <= f(x, y)$. As a result, $z = f(x, y)$ must be greater than zero everywhere for the flat-bottomed (thick = 0) version. A model will still be produced if there are z values that are less than zero, but it will be an invalid model, and even if you manage to repair it, it won't print easily.

Listing 1-1. The Basic OpenSCAD Model to Create a 3D Print of a Surface

```
// OpenSCAD model to print out an arbitrary surface defined as z = f(x,y)
// Either prints the surface as two sided and variable thick = thickness
// Or if thick = 0, prints a top surface with a flat bottom
// File surfaceprint.scad

function f(x, y) = ((x - 50) * (y - 50)) / 100 + 30; // Saddle point

//z height, in mm

thick = 0; //set to 0 for flat bottom. else mm thickness of surface
xmax = 99; //Number of points in x direction - 99 is the max
ymax = 99; // Number of points in y direction - 99 is the max

// If you want a rough surface (to make it more tactile) set blocky=true.
// Otherwise surface will be smoothed
blocky = false; //if true, xmax and ymax must be less than 100.

//number of points that will be plotted
toppoints = (xmax + 1) * (ymax + 1);
```

```
//next section generates the points in the array
points = concat(
    [for(y = [0:ymax], x = [0:xmax]) [x, y, f(x, y)]], // top face
    (thick ? //bottom face
        [for(y = [0:ymax], x = [0:xmax]) [x, y, f(x, y) - thick]] :
        [for(y = [0:ymax], x = [0:xmax]) [x, y, 0]]
    )
);

zbounds = [min([for(i = points) i[2]]), max([for(i = points) i[2]])];

//create triangles from quad
function quad(a, b, c, d, r = false) = r ? [[a, b, c], [c, d, a]] : [[c, b, a],
[a, d, c]];

faces = concat(
    //build top and bottom
        [for(bottom = [0, toppoints], i = [for(x = [0:xmax - 1], y = [0:ymax - 1])
            quad(
                x + (xmax + 1) * (y + 1) + bottom,
                x + (xmax + 1) * y + bottom,
                x + 1 + (xmax + 1) * y + bottom,
                x + 1 + (xmax + 1) * (y + 1) + bottom,
                bottom
            )], v = i) v],
        [for(i = [for(x = [0, xmax], y = [0:ymax - 1]) //build left and right
            quad(
                x + (xmax + 1) * y + toppoints,
                x + (xmax + 1) * y,
                x + (xmax + 1) * (y + 1),
                x + (xmax + 1) * (y + 1) + toppoints,
                x
            )], v = i) v],
        [for(i = [for(x = [0:xmax - 1], y = [0, ymax]) //build front and back
            quad(
                x + (xmax + 1) * y + toppoints,
                x + 1 + (xmax + 1) * y+ toppoints,
                x + 1 + (xmax + 1) * y,
                x + (xmax + 1) * y,
                y
            )], v = i) v]
);

//Now either generate the surface as discrete cuboids
// or smoothly with the polyhedron function
```

```
if(blocky) for(i = [0:toppoints - 1]) translate(points[toppoints + i])
cube([1.001, 1.001, points[i][2] - points[toppoints + i][2]]);
else polyhedron(points, faces);

echo(zbounds);
```

Printing Considerations

Since this model was designed to have a flat bottom, it prints easily. There will not be any overhangs. If your function would get very tall, you may want to scale it down by multiplying the equation by a constant. To check that the function is not getting too big or going negative in the z direction, you can either just run it in OpenSCAD and look at the result, or graph it conventionally yourself to see what it looks like. (The model does not check it for you.)

Limitations and Alternatives

To keep the model simple, transparent, and easy to understand, we have not inserted any error checking or special cases. Obviously, if you have a function that goes to infinity or has some sort of discontinuity, you will need to come up with some fix. You could, for example, create a branch in the definition of $f(x, y)$ to handle cases that are poorly behaved in the mathematical sense.

We could only test a few cases, and there are an infinite number of options, so as with any print you should check the software model of your print before committing it to be sure that it worked for your particular example. As discussed earlier, z has to be greater than zero.

Another parameter in the code is blocky, which in this example is set to false. Setting blocky = true will create a slightly rough-textured surface instead of the smooth one here, which generally will take a lot longer to render in OpenSCAD—we have pulled out this code in a later section as a freestanding tiny model, so you might want to try using it that way.

■ **Caution** OpenSCAD's math functions will probably look familiar if you are a programmer, but some of them will not be what you are expecting if you do not have that experience already. Exponents, for example, take the form of pow(base, exponent) rather than using a superscript, and a square root uses the sqrt() function instead of a radical sign. You can find a (nearly) complete listing of the mathematical functions available in OpenSCAD at https://en.wikibooks.org/wiki/OpenSCAD_User_Manual/Mathematical_Functions.

Making a Two-Sided Smoothed Surface

Although it is convenient to be able to visualize the top of a surface in 3D, sometimes it is even better to see it from both sides. However, you might think that then you will have to put a lot of support under the surface and wind up more or less with the same thing. The way out of this is to print the surface *sideways*. As long as the surface does not contain slopes that are too steep, you can use the following process to print a surface that is a few mm thick (2 mm in this example, the minimum we recommend) and print it *on its side*.

Run the same model in OpenSCAD as in the previous section (after changing the thick parameter to equal the desired thickness in mm), scale it if you like (be sure the thickness does not go below 2 mm), and rotate it 90 degrees about either the *x* or *y* axis. Look at your model to determine which rotation will have the fewest overhangs. If the excursions in $f(x, y)$ were big, you might have to use some support this way but probably far less than if you laid the surface flat. As a bonus, *z* can be negative in this version.

■ **Tip** For stability, it is wise to add some material to the platform in the first layer around the print. Your software may call this a *brim;* if you are not given the option of using a brim, use a skirt zero distance from the print instead, which is equivalent. Figure 1-2 shows the skirt in MatterControl; we told the software to use a five-loop skirt and to place it 0 mm away.

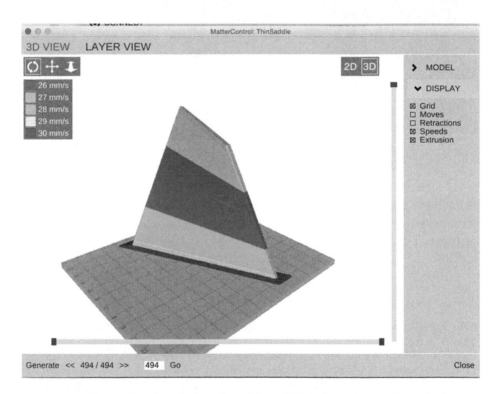

Figure 1-2. *The simulated vertical version of the saddle surface in MatterControl. The brim is the wider are surrounding the first layer on the build platform. Shading (color in ebook) show different print speeds*

The only difference between this case and the previous section is that the parameter thick was a nonzero positive number. In this case, we set it to 4. Thus, we generated a file that had the dimensions 99 by 99 mm in *x* and *y*, and was 4 mm thick in *z*. We decided that was bigger than we wanted to print, so we scaled down to half size in MatterControl (thus leaving it 49.5 mm by 49.5 mm by 2 mm thick.) Figure 1-3 shows the finished print still on the printer, held down in part by its attached skirt.

Figure 1-3. *The saddle surface print as it finished*

■ **Caution**   If you scale the surface, you have to be sure that the piece remains at least 2 mm or so thick after scaling. If you want something about 50 mm across, for example, and will be scaling it down by a factor of 2, you should start with thick = 4.

Very Simple Model to Make a "Blocky" One-Sided Surface

Sometimes there are advantages to having a surface that is a bit rough. You might want to be able to feel the shape more, or you might want it to be a little more matte finish. The model in Listing 1-2 is an extremely simple one that will create an STL file with a surface of small cubical pieces. Rather than using triangular faces to interpolate as we did in the other model, this leaves the surface elements discretized. You are just creating *xmax* + 1 times *ymax* + 1 rectangular solids 1 mm by 1 mm by *f*(*x, y*) high. The blocky = true setting in Listing 1-1 produces the same result, but we have pulled it out and simplified it here for discussion purposes, and to give you something simpler to play with on your own. It is slower than the model in Listing 1-1 (with blocky = false) for most cases, but its very simplicity may give you some ideas of things you may want to try.

Figure 1-4 shows a surface generated this way. OpenSCAD can take a while to render 100 by 100 surfaces this way.

Listing 1-2. OpenSCAD Model to Generate a "Blocky" Surface

```
// Model to generate a simple, "blocky" file
// File name: BlockyMath.scad
function f(x, y) = ((x - 50) * (y - 50)) / 100 + 30; xmax = 20;
ymax = 20;
for(x = [0:xmax], y = [0:ymax]) translate([x, y, 0]) cube([1.001, 1.001, f(x, y)]);
```

Figure 1-4. *The blocky surface, as printed, scaled by 2 in the x and y direction, original scaling in z*

Creating Surfaces from an External Data File

The processes we have used in the chapter so far have the virtue that everything was controlled entirely within OpenSCAD. However, since OpenSCAD does not have variables in the normal coding sense of the word, it is hard to do things like scale the surface dynamically or do any of the other things you might want to do for a complex mathematical model. (OpenSCAD has variables as a mathematician might think of them—what most programming languages would call *constants*.) You might have another piece of software creating your surface data points, and all you want to do is essentially plot them out as a 3D surface, either with a flat base or as a thin surface.

In this section, we use OpenSCAD's *surface* module to plot a file of points generated by a program in the common language Python. There is nothing special about using Python versus C or any other language, but it does happen to be a language often used by scientists, so we felt it was appropriate here. The only critical thing is that the language needs to be able to create a text file in a format we will get to shortly. You could use a spreadsheet or for that matter a text editor to create your file of values.

Example: Using a Python Program to Generate Data for a Thin Surface

Listing 1-3 is a file Joan created in the Apple Python 2.7.8 Integrated Development Environment (IDE) that creates a 100 by 100 point matrix of two superposed radial cosine waves and stores it in the file sinusoids.dat. It is creating a file of datapoints for the surface

$$z = 2 \cos(\pi\, r_1/5) + 2 \cos(\pi\, r_2/5) + 6$$

where r_1 is a radial distance centered on $x = 50$ and $y = 50$ (1 mm from the center of Figures 1-5 and 1-6) and r_2 is a radial distance centered on $x = 0$, $y = 0$ (defined as the lower right-hand corner of the pieces in this section). The offset of 6 ensures that the surface will always be at least 2 mm thick, since the other two terms are at a minimum a sum equal to –4.

Listing 1-3. Python Code to Create a File for Surface Creation

```
# JH August 17, 2015 - example for open scad surface test
import math
import sys
f = open('sinusoids.dat', 'w');

# Create a 10 by 10 matrix of two interfering sinusoids
# And saves it in the file opened above
# Each data point by default creates a 1 mm square base voxel

pi = 4. * math.atan(1.);
print('pi is ', pi);
numx = 100;
numy = 100;

for x_index in range(0, numx):
  for y_index in range(0, numy):
    xcenter1 = x_index;
    xcenter2 = x_index - 50;
    ycenter1 = y_index;
    ycenter2 = y_index - 50;
```

```
      radius1 = 0.2*pi* math.sqrt((xcenter1 * xcenter1) + (ycenter1 * ycenter1));
      radius2 = 0.2*pi*math.sqrt((xcenter2 * xcenter2 ) + (ycenter2 * ycenter2));
      fxy = 2.0* math.cos(radius1) + 2 * math.cos(radius2) + 6;
      f.write(str(fxy) + ' ');
    f.write('\n');
f.close();
```

Figure 1-5. *The model as it was being printed, showing the skirt (extra plastic where the object meets the build platform)*

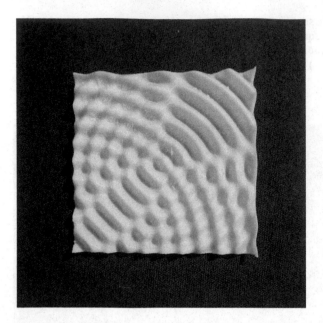

Figure 1-6. *The model after it finished printing. (0, 0) is on the lower left*

■ **Note**   There are many versions of Python available for free. If you want to look up the functions discussed so far, you can find good documentation at `https://docs.python.org/2/index.html`. Mac computers with OS X above version 10.3 come bundled with Python, and various free versions are available for Windows computers.

The code in Listing 1-3 creates a file in the same directory as the code file. Then we created a model in OpenSCAD, which also had to run in the same directory. (We could have created a full directory path for it, but chose not to.) Listing 1-4 shows this model.

Listing 1-4. The OpenSCAD Model That Takes Python Input

```
// Model to take externally-generated surface data
// And to then create a surface in OpenSCAD with it
// File SurfaceFromData.scad
difference() {
    translate([0, 0, 2]) surface(file = "sinusoids.dat", center = true,
convexity = 5);
    surface(file = "sinusoids.dat", center = true, convexity = 5);
}
```

This says to print the data in the file sinusoids.dat and center the surface at (0, 0) and specifies a parameter that affects how the surface is viewed in OpenSCAD itself (without bearing on the final transformation into a printable file). Then we subtract away a surface 2 mm away, which leaves a surface 2 mm thick.

Constraints

The two surfaces have to have a clean 2 mm offset from each other or this does not work. The value of *fxy* in Listing 1-3 has to be greater than the offset value in Listing 1-4, so you will need to add an offset to *fxy* to keep it from going below the offset (here, the offset used was 2).

Figure 1-5 shows the model nearing completion (it was rotated so that (0, 0) wound up in the upper left, as seen there), and Figure 1-6 shows it completed. There was some stringing from lack of support in this orientation, but not disastrously so. If you had a surface that had a minimum value that was less obvious than the example just given, you could of course compute your points, find the minimum, and apply an offset such that every data point had a *z* value of at least the planned thickness of the surface. In this example, we are creating a surface that is 100 mm by 100 mm and 2 mm thick. If the *z* value is less than that, one side of the surface may be clipped when you print it.

■ **Note** The format that OpenSCAD expects for its surface function is a text file with values in a row separated by spaces, with a newline at the end of each row. OpenSCAD's surface module will create a shape using the *z* values from the file in a 1mm grid, just like that in Listing 1-1. Values need to be greater than zero for reliable results.

THINKING ABOUT THESE MODELS: LEARNING LIKE A MAKER

In each chapter of this book, we will talk a little about what we learned while we were developing the models, so that you can think a little about what you would like to do with them. This chapter is a little different from the rest in that the models here are an underlying tool that is useful for many of the other chapters of the book. In Chapter 2, for example, we will explore waves and fields, and will draw on the ability to plot out 3D functions that are usually shown as 2D projections.

In our case, we had to think hard about what types of functions would most usefully be visualized this way and how to balance an overly complex model that would be hard for you to alter versus a reasonably capable one. After a lot of experimentation, we came up with the set described here. We encourage you to play with them and let us know what else you come up with. (See Appendix A for information about how to contribute to the open source repository of these models.)

Finally, we have been surprised at how much mathematical insight comes about through first thinking about how to create the model and then handling the finished product. Just flipping over a sinusoid (as in the last example) leads you to ask a lot of questions about how the different sinusoidal functions are related.

We found as we worked on some of the models later in this book that often everyone uses the same 2D projection of a 3D model, and that actually creating the entire model literally gives you a different perspective. Figure 1-7 shows all the objects in this chapter together. It is a bit of an exercise in seeing how different a 2D photograph can make a 3D surface look; with the models in hand, we really struggled to arrange them to make it clear what shape they were and what the scale of any imperfections was, relative to the object itself.

Figure 1-7. *All the models from this chapter together for comparison*

Where to Learn More

There are obviously many different sites to learn about the mathematics of the example functions shown in this chapter. Joan's personal favorite place to send students to learn more about math (but not tied to 3D printing) is the Kahn Academy, at www.khanacademy.org.

If you want to see some other 3D-printed mathematics, have a look at the sites of Elizabeth Denne (of Washington and Lee University), which mostly use Mathematica for modeling:

http://mathvis.academic.wlu.edu
http://home.wlu.edu/~dennee/math_vis.html
http://www.thingiverse.com/dennedesigns/about

Sculptors Bathsheba Grossman and Henry Segerman create mathematics-based sculpture, available at their respective sites www.bathsheba.com and www.shapeways.com/shops/henryseg. Paul Nylander (http://bugman123.com) has a variety of math- and science-oriented models on his site. And of course, you can always search on the various websites of 3D models (such as www.thingiverse.com/explore/newest/learning/math and www.youmagine.com) for math models.

Teacher Tips

In later chapters, we give some suggestions about alignments to science standards. Here, rather than give an enormous list of possible links, we will just note that pretty much any level of math that can benefit from tactile demonstrations can be served by prints created by this software, and the science that uses that mathematics can benefit similarly. (For example, in Chapter 2 we show how to use some of these surfaces to visualize light waves and gravity fields.)

We intended these model for surfaces that are difficult to visualize and that can be hard to think about in projected form, but you may find someone in one of your classes at any level who will find a 3D model can break a logjam. At the simplest level, you can print out sample functions with a few parameters changed and have durable visualization tools that can survive being passed around a classroom.

Science Fair Project Ideas

If you decide you want to have a 3D-printed mathematical function as part of a project, you will discover that you think differently about a math function when you are considering how to display it in 3D versus using the same 2D illustration that everyone else uses. Consider, for example, printing out a model of a function that applies to your product and taking measurements off it with a pair of calipers to see whether it agrees with theory. See if the creation of the physical model and any issues you had while printing give you insight into the problem.

Summary

In this chapter, you learned several different ways to create a 3D model of a mathematical function in the OpenSCAD 3D solid modeling program, either one-sided on a flat base or as a thin two-sided sheet. You also saw how to create a file with an external program (Python code in the example) to pass through OpenSCAD, in case you are generating surfaces in other codes and would like 3D models of them. Finally, we gave you a few pointers to places to see more math examples and some ways to use these models in teaching and science fairs.

CHAPTER 2

■ ■ ■

Light and Other Waves

When someone says "waves," the first thing that may come to mind is the kind of waves that crash onto a beach. Water waves (and waves in air) are actually pretty complicated, because the waves are moving over complex terrrain, experiencing friction and effects of the water's viscosity and a lot of other things. The equations that govern water waves and the interactions among them require that you know about a type of math called *partial differential equations*, which even scientists and engineers might not work with much until graduate school.

Fortunately, though, light waves and other electromagnetic radiation follow some rules that simplify a lot of things for some special cases. The geometries of even these simpler interacting wave examples can be pretty complicated, though. In this chapter, we will develop some 3D-printable models that represent some of these special cases to help you visualize wave interactions. Students at all levels have trouble visualizing the properties of light and magnetism because of their abstract nature; if you are a teacher, you may find some of these materials useful just to pass around while discussing some of these phenomena.

This chapter assumes you are pretty comfortable with trigonometric functions like *sine, cosine,* and *tangent* and their inverses (*asin, acos, atan*). We also talk about the $sinc(x)$ function, which is just $sinc(x) = sin(x)/x$, defined as equal to 1 if $x = 0$. (Since 0/0 is always "undefined" mathematically, a definition is needed for the function to have a value right at $x = 0$—otherwise it would approach 1 as x got small, but never quite get there.) Some types of engineers define $sinc(x)$ differently, so be sure you are using the one shown here.

We will explore some topics that are typically taught at levels from high school through the research level, and the eager student will have a lot of places they can go exploring further. (The authors would like to acknowledge the assistance of astronomer and interferometry expert Stephen Unwin in clarifying the physics underlying this chapter and suggesting good ways to frame some of the basics without resorting to calculus.)

■ **Note**   Everything in this chapter is generated with OpenSCAD for modeling and MatterControl for controlling the printer. The demonstration prints illustrated in this chapter were done on a Deezmaker Bukito printer, using PLA plastic, with 0.2 mm layer height and no support other than a brim (or attached skirt, if you prefer to think of it that way) to glue down the first layer.

Physics and Math Background

The models in this chapter are two-dimensional waves (in the x/y plane). We show their amplitude as the model's height in the z direction. In the case of a water wave, the height of the water wave would be the z value. For a light wave, it is better to think of the height (value of z) as the brightness of the light at that x, y position at a snapshot in time. In some other cases, we will calculate the square of the amplitude and display that as the z value. That can be thought of as the average over time of the waves passing through that point in space, since the waves are propagating over time. We show them in the models in this chapter as just functions of space—a snapshot at a particular time, or an average over time, as the case may be.

Coordinate System and Conventions

For all the models in this chapter, we used *xmax* and *ymax* set to 99 (see Listing 1-1). This means that the models are all 100 by 100 points and by default will print out 100 by 100 mm (about 4 inches square, with thickness depending on other parameters that we describe for each case). More points are usually better, but more points can make the OpenSCAD model take a very long time to render and require you to do some scaling down unless you have a very big printer. This value seems to be a good tradeoff that keeps feature size big enough to be printed while preserving the important features. You will need to play with this a little as you develop models.

The origin is at the lower right-hand corner, and x and y are both always positive and go from 0 to 99. Some of the models add an offset to the z value to make printing possible (since 3D printers usually have a convention that $z = 0$ is the printer's build platform, so nothing can be printed with a negative z value).

As we will talk about later in the chapter, we will not normally 3D print these models such that the x and y axes of the models are printed aligned with the x and y plane (parallel to the build platform) of the 3D printer. When we talk about x, y, and z in this chapter, we mean the coordinates of the model.

Finally, OpenSCAD uses degrees in its trigonometric functions. In most of our illustrations, we talk about angles in radians, since that is how most textbooks present the problems, and also because it works out conveniently in many more advanced topics, should you choose to keep going. We note conversions as we go.

■ **Note**　We replaced the function $f(x,y)$ used in Listing 1-1 to generate the models in this chapter. We give you just the model for the function (sometimes, several interrelated functions) in this chapter to avoid repeating the same model over and over. The downloadable model versions include the entire model in each file, incorporating both the function $f(x,y)$ here plus the rest of the Listing 1-1 material. Comments in the model and shown here may vary somewhat for clarity and context.

Principle of Superposition

Imagine that you are on a still pond and you start poking a stick in and out of the water. Ripples will spread across the pond. Then suppose a friend nearby started doing the same thing. The ripples going in multiple directions would in some cases add up (creating a doubly-high ripple) and in others, subtract or cancel out.

In real life, the waves on the pond will die out and have other complex interactions, but we can get a lot of insight into many kinds of *electromagnetic* waves (like light and radio waves) by modeling the waves as simple sine and cosine waves that interact with each other like the ripples you just imagined on the pond.

For many kinds of waves, you can add the effects of the different waves, called the *principle of superposition* (https://en.wikipedia.org/wiki/Superposition_principle). When the waves add, it is called *constructive* interference; when they cancel each other out, it is *destructive* interference. We will use this principle, and an adaptation of the model from Listing 1-1, to visualize some classic experiments.

Some Basic Examples

To give you some feel for how different types of wave geometries might play out, we walk through a couple of examples. One of the things that this model makes very easy is putting together fairly complex combinations of sinusoids and seeing the wave interactions. As discussed later in the chapter, we will be simplifying some of the physics behind some of the wave phenomena we model, but you can still gain some good insight from playing with these models.

Point Sources and Plane Waves

This section looks at point sources, which put energy into a system in a concentrated way—sort of like the stick in the water we talked about earlier, or a small bright light in a big room. Energy from that source would then go out in all directions radially from the point. The other basic type of wave we talk about is a *plane wave*—a straight line wave across the whole plane, like waves far out at sea. Then we look how these appear when they are superposed on each other.

Listing 2-1 gives the OpenSCAD model for an overlap of the two types of waves. The plane wave has four times the amplitude of the radial source, and a *wavelength* five times as long. In Figure 2-1 you can see what a snapshot of this looks like when 3D printed. The print is 100 mm square and 3 mm thick. The waves going from left to right (that is, traveling in the x direction) are bigger and farther apart than the short ripples from the point source on the left, which is centered at the point (49.5, 49.5).

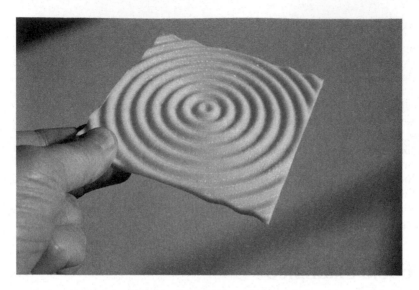

Figure 2-1. *Just the point source radiating from the center*

The model assumes that you are calculating a value for the combined waves at each point (x,y) on a square grid going from (0,0) to (99,99). However, many of the functions are in terms of the distance from a source to a particular point in space. We calculate that distance in the function radius, which calculates the distance from the source at (xc,yc) to the point (x,y). Figure 2-1 shows just the point source; Figure 2-2, just the plane wave; and Figure 2-3, the two superposed.

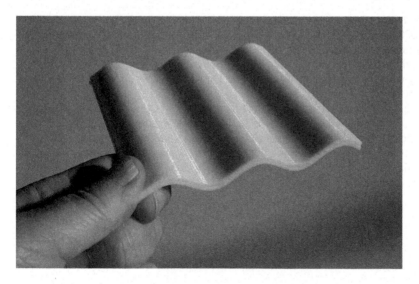

Figure 2-2. *The plane wave alone*

Figure 2-3. *Plane wave and point source interaction*

■ **Note** OpenSCAD assumes degrees in all its trigonometric functions, and here radians are far more convenient. 2π radians = 360 degrees. This requires multiplying by $2\pi/360$, or $\pi/180$, quite often in what follows. We show the equations in the form that assumes radians, since it is much simpler to understand. The two waves being superposed in Listing 2-1 are calculated in *degrees*. In radians, the first term would be cos($5r/6$) and the second term, 4*sin($r/6$).

Listing 2-1. Function for Superposition of Radial and Plane Wave

```
// File basicWaves.scad
function radius(x,y, xc, yc) = sqrt( (x-xc)*(x-xc) + (y-yc)*(y-yc) );
function f(x, y) =  cos((150/PI)*radius(x,y,49.5, 49.5) )  + 4* sin( (30/PI)*x) +5;
 thick = 3; //set to 0 for flat bottom. else mm thickness of surface
```

Two Interacting Sources

What happens if we have two interacting point sources at one edge of the plane we are modeling? The model for that is given in Listing 2-2, and the model we printed is in Figure 2-4. In this case, we are printing a model in which *z* represents the square of the amplitude of the sum of the waves generated by these two sources. As we will see in the next section, this is also an equivalent of the time average of the intensity pattern that

21

would be generated by a wave passing through two infinitely thin, infinitely long slits oriented at right angles to the print and located at $x = xc1$ and $xc2$. In the next section, we will see what happens when they are *not* infinitely thin slits.

Figure 2-4. *The square of the combined amplitudes of two point sources sending out waves radially on one plane, with a wavelength of 4 mm. The (0,0) point is on the upper right; the sources are just above the person's thumb, on the edge of the model*

In Listing 2-2, lambda is the wavelength, in mm; r is the distance (also in mm) from the center of each of the point sources to the point (x,y) on the surface; and factor is an arbitrary scaling factor to adjust how large the features are. Note that the equations are in radians because that is how they are shown in most physics books, but since OpenSCAD uses degrees, we needed to convert from the equation to its encoding.

We would need to use some calculus concepts to prove this, but generally speaking, the square of the amplitude is proportional to the average amplitude of a wave moving over a surface over time. We will use that smoothed average in the next section, so we do it here as well so that we can compare the results later.

■ **Note** Raising a variable to a power in OpenSCAD uses the pow function, so pow(x,2) would return *x* squared.

Listing 2-2. Function for Superposition of Two Point Sources

```
// file multipleWaves.scad
factor =1;
lambda=4;
xc1 = 49.5 -10;
xc2 = 49.5 + 10;
function radius(x,y, xc, yc) = sqrt( (x-xc)*(x-xc) + (y-yc)*(y-yc) );
function f(x, y) =  factor* pow ( (cos( (360/lambda)*radius(x,y,xc1,0 )
            + cos( (360/lambda)*radius(x,y,xc2,0) ),2) +2;
//You are computing sin ( (2*PI/lambda) * (180/PI) r)
//Equation above simplifies to get (360*r/lambda). OpenSCAD presumes degrees.
thick = 0; //set to 0 for flat bottom. else mm thickness of surface
```

■ **Caution**   Some of the fine structure in Figure 2-4 is just an artifact of the sampling rate being too low for the given wavelength. We are *sampling* (creating a surface data point) every 1 mm, and the wavelength is only 4 mm. Given the averaging used in the model that creates the surface, this is not quite enough. We created this for comparison with later discussions of two finite slits. The finite slit case is a function of a particular angular maeasurement (and is not a snapshot in time as these are) and is not as vulnerable to these issues. Figure 2-5 shows the same surface with a wavelength four times as long (and sources 36 mm apart instead of 20).

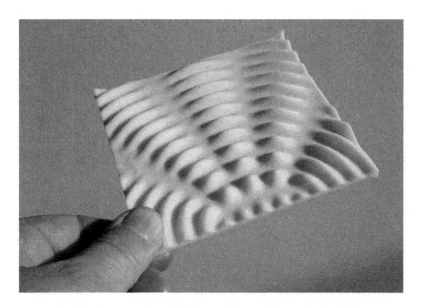

Figure 2-5. *Longer wavelength version of Figure 2-4, with slits farther apart*

More Complex Examples: Diffraction

We can combine some of these ideas to create some models of the phenomenon of *diffraction* (https://en.wikipedia.org/wiki/Diffraction). Waves *diffract,* changing their geometry and how they interact with each other when they encounter a physical barrier of some kind. What happens when a wave front passes through a wall with either one or two slits in it and contines through on the other side? In 1803 Thomas Young performed his double-slit experiment to try and quantify what the pattern of bright and dark areas would be if someone were to hold up a screen after the light had passed through these slits (see https://en.wikipedia.org/wiki/Young's_interference_experiment for more). A note, though: here we are showing a monochromatic (one wavelength of simulated light) version of the experiment. The original experiment used multiple wavelengths and produced a rainbow interference pattern.

The Double-Slit Experiment

Figure 2-6 shows the setup of Young's double-slit experiment, arranged the way we will refer to the various aspects of it in this section. The two slits are assumed to be larger than the wavelength of the light passing through them, close together relative to the overall area we are modeling. The angle θ is the angle between a light ray to a given point (x,y) and the vertical. A light wave from a source below the bottom of Figure 2-6 would shine through the two slits and then interact.

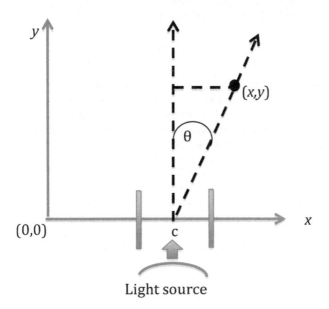

Figure 2-6. *The double-slit experimental setup, along with some of the models from this chapter*

Young found that what he saw were alternating light and dark bands on a screen behind his slits, showing how the wave front going through each slit interfered constructively and destructively at different points in space. This experiment was taken as proof that light travels in waves that can be added together to produce *interference patterns*. How the high and low areas of our 3D-printed models line up with the experiment's geometry is shown in Figure 2-3 (except that the amplitude would be in the *z* direction, out of the page.)

Listing 2-3. Model for Two Slits

```
//File twoSlits.scad
lambda = 4; //wavelength, same units as slit
slit = lambda * 2; // width of slit
slit_separation = lambda* 4; //distance between slits
c = 49.5; //center of slit pair
factor = 20; //scaling factor, for visiblity
```

```
function sintheta(x,y) =  (x-c)/sqrt ( (x-c) * (x-c) + y*y);
function slit_sinc(x,y) =  lambda*sin (180*sintheta(x,y) * slit/lambda)/
(PI*slit*sintheta(x,y) );
 // note PI/PI goes away inside sin
function slit_cos(x,y) = cos (180*sintheta(x,y) * slit_separation/lambda);
function f(x,y) =  factor * pow(slit_sinc(x,y), 2)* pow(slit_cos(x,y),2)+2;
 //This function is now the DUAL-slit experiment.
 // sinc squared of ( slit * pi* sin (theta)/lambda)
thick = 0; //set to 0 for flat bottom. else mm thickness of surface
```

One-Slit Examples

Light passing through just one slit in a similar setup gives a spread-out illuminated area after the light passes through the slit. For one slit, the equation for the intensity is proportional to $\mathrm{sinc}^2(\pi\, d \sin\theta/\lambda)$ and for two slits, to $\cos^2(\pi\, b \sin\theta/\lambda)\, \mathrm{sinc}^2(\pi\, d \sin\theta/\lambda)$; $\mathrm{sinc}(x)$ is defined as $\sin(x)/x$ unless $x = 0$, in which case $\mathrm{sinc}(0) = 1$. Here d is the width of each slit, b is the distance between them, λ (the Greek letter lambda) is the wavelength, and θ (Greek letter theta) is the angle defined in Figure 2-6. This works out to the two-slit intensity being the intensity pattern from one slit multiplied by a (squared) cosine wave.

If you look at the models in Figures 2-7 and 2-8 you can see these patterns. We created a "negative space" version of the one-slit case so we could explore how well it fits over the two-slit case. In Figure 2-8 you can see that it does indeed fit pretty well. OpenSCAD functions for each of the objects shown in Figure 2-8 are in Listing 2-3 (two slits), Listing 2-4 (one slit), and Listing 2-5 (one-slit negative space).

Figure 2-7. *Model of light through one slit (positive, left, and inverted, center) and two slits (right). Illumination at the top as shown here*

Figure 2-8. *One-slit intensity function (left) and the negative-space version over the two-slit one*

In Listing 2-4 we have a function sintheta(x,y). This function computes the sine of the angle theta (θ) from the geometry. Do not be confused by the lack of a call to the sin() function. Here we just go back to sine being opposite over hypoteneuse, as shown in in Figure 2-6.

Listing 2-4. Model for One Slit

```
//File oneSlit.scad
lambda =4; //wavelength, same units as slit
slit = 8; // width of slit
c = 49.5; //center of slit
factor=20; //scaling factor, for visiblity
function sinetheta(x,y) =  (x-c)/ sqrt ( (x-c) * (x-c) + y*y);
function slit_sinc(x,y) =  lambda*sin (180*sinetheta(x,y) * slit/lambda)/
(PI*slit*sinetheta(x,y)); // note PI/PI goes away inside sin
function f(x,y) =  factor * pow(slit_sinc(x,y), 2) +2;
  //This function is now the SINGLE-slit experiment.
 // sinc squared of ( slit * pi* sin (theta)/lambda)
thick = 0; //set to 0 for flat bottom. else mm thickness of surface
```

Listing 2-5. Model for the "Empty Space" Inverse of the One Slit Case

```
//File inverseOneSlit.scad
lambda =4; //wavelength, same units as slit
slit = 8; // width of slit
c = 49.5; //center of slit
factor=20; //scaling factor, for visiblity
function sinetheta(x,y) =  (x-c)/ sqrt ( (x-c) * (x-c) + y*y);
function slit_sinc(x,y) =  lambda*sin (180*sinetheta(x,y) *
slit/lambda)/(PI*slit*sinetheta(x,y)); // note PI/PI goes away inside sin
```

```
// This function is now the SINGLE-slit experiment, inverted
// (to show how other cases fit into it)
function f(x,y) = 24-factor * pow(slit_sinc(x,y), 2) ; //for inverse version
 // sinc squared of ( slit * pi* sin (theta)/lambda)
thick = 0; //set to 0 for flat bottom. else mm thickness of surface
```

■ **Caution**   In these models we cheated a little by avoiding situations where we would need to compute sinc(0), which is defined as equal to 1. (It is 0/0 otherwise.)

Figure 2-9 gives a top view of the one-slit intensity pattern (inverted, top left; positive, bottom left), the double-slit (top right), and the two infinitely thin slits spaced the same as the finite ones (bottom left). In all cases, they were printed with thick=0 (flat bottoms). The equations used are *far field* equations (known as Fraunhofer diffraction) and do not really apply right at the slits. You see some artifacts if you look closely.

Figure 2-9. *Inverted one slit (top L), two slits (top R), one slit (bottom L), and two point sources spaced the same as the slits and using the same wavelength (bottom R)*

Applying this phenomenon for useful purposes is called *interferometry*. It has many applications in fields ranging from astronomy to manufacturing; we discuss some of them in the "Where to Learn More" section later in this chapter.

Printing Considerations

You may have been wondering how we were 3D printing the wave patterns when `thick` was not equal to zero (that is, when we did not have a flat bottom). Actually, all the objects in this chapter have been printed sideways. Figure 2-10 shows two of the objects (that *did* have `thick=0`) as they were printed. Depending on the orientation that will have the fewest overhangs, you may want to rotate the object in *x* or *y* plus or minus 90 degrees to get to this point.

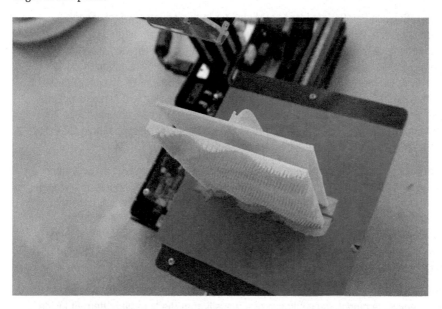

Figure 2-10. *The infinitely thin pair of slits and the two finite slits printing at the same time*

The other advantage of printing these functions vertically is that fine detail will print much better. If you had details with a lot of gaps between them, like the two point sources example (back in Figure 2-2), you will get a lot of stringing if you try to print a layer with a lot of gaps. But printing it vertically means that each layer essentially has no gaps on the surface perimeter, and just internal ones for the infill layers.

The print will stick well if you use a skirt that has four or five loops around the base, and is zero distance away, equivalent to a brim (different 3D-printing software refers to these differently.) You may want to have a wider and slower first layer extrusion.

THINKING ABOUT THESE MODELS: LEARNING LIKE A MAKER

When we started working on this chapter, we found ourselves asking a lot of fundamental questions about what we were trying to represent, and which models would give the most insight. One of the challenges here was that waves normally propagate in space *and* time, so in some ways a 3D model has the same issues as a 2D video simulation. You have three dimensions, but either it has to be a snapshot in time or one of the spatial axes needs to represent something other than the third dimension. Thinking about that and when it is worthwhile to have a "two-sided" model took a lot of time and discussion with several physicists.

In the "Science Fair Project Ideas" section later in this chapter, we talk about magnetism and why we decided not to include any models of magnetic fields. Magnetic fields were more difficult to think about in many ways because the magnetic fields have both a magnitude and a direction, which is difficult to show in a 3D static model. We explored models of simple bar magnets, as well as those of Earth's magnetic field and of the Sun. However, very few simple equation solutions give very much insight, and many field equations are in very inconvenient (for 3D printing) polar coordinate systems. Others are designed for a static simple case that gives one number—not a very interesting 3D print.

A little digging revealed that as a practical matter many people who actually need to model these things rely on one of several semi-experimental models. It seemed to us like there were not a lot of models for which a surface without directional markings would be an improvement to a 2D drawing with arrows showing the field direction. However, we included it in the "Science Fair" section so that more advanced students might consider whether a simplified model, applied thoughtfully, might be interesting to explore a narrow hypothesis.

One of the things that came up with the set of models for this chapter was the idea of an *envelope model*. You could see pretty easily that the two-slit pattern fit inside the envelope created by the one-slit case, but creating a "negative space" model so that the two could actually be fit together was really interesting. We encourage you to think about other applications of this and places where it might give you more insight. Basically all you do is subtract the function of interest from a number big enough so that the negative space "fits inside" an outer box; see Figures 2-7 through 2-9 and Listing 2-5.

Because we elected not to use any math here beyond high school–level geometry and trigonometry, some of the discussion of the amplitude of the waves or why you may want to look at the square of the amplitude for a time average are of necessity a little vague and ignore some dependencies on time, frequency, and other things that are important in real applications. If you need to go beyond these rough conceptual ideas, be sure you know the equations governing your case and when the simplistic approach here is appropriate and when it is not.

Where to Learn More

Good general background on the topics in this chapter can be found at the Khan Academy (www.khanacademy.org/science/physics/light-waves) and many articles on Wikipedia. A good introductory college-level physics or electrical engineering textbook will help for the next level of exploration beyond what we have here.

The material in this chapter could be taken many different directions. We have not even touched on the many electrical engineering applications of *Fourier Transforms*, a technique that uses the mathematics of combining waves to solve engineering problems (https://en.wikipedia.org/wiki/Fourier_transform).

The properties of interfering waves are used routinely in applications that require a lot of precision. Astronomers use radio interferometry to create images of objects that, as they would say, *subtend* a small angle in the sky. This can either be something small that is sort of far away, or something big that is very, very far away. Astronomers make interferometry observations by taking signals from two radio telescopes (those big dishes like those seen in the movie *Contact*, for instance) and thinking of the two telescopes as two slits admitting light from a point source very far away (in this case, it might be another galaxy).

The farther away the telescopes are from each other, the finer the detail of the object that can be taken from the radio waves. If there are groups of telescopes at different distances from each other, an image can be built up from the signals of different resolution of the same object. The VLA (Very Large Array, www.vla.nrao.edu) in Socorro, New Mexico, was designed for this application with 27 radio telescopes arranged in a Y-shaped configuration.

A nearer-to-home application is laser interferometry for precise measurement of optical and other precision surfaces that are being machined. Laser beams interfere with each other when the surface is shaped correctly, and so the pattern from a test beam and one reflecting off the surface will give information about surface inaccuracies.

Teacher Tips

Waves in fluids are taught at various points in the K-12 curriculum. Light waves are dealt with in a somewhat cursory way, since as noted earlier many properties of waves cannot be fully appreciated until students have had some exposure to undergraduate-level physics and math.

However, playing with these models to build some intuiton can motivate learning about some of the precursor material or lead to science-fair or extra-credit projects. That said, if you enter "waves" on the Next Generation Science standards website (www.nextgenscience.org) you will get a lot of hits. Here are some we thought might be particularly good places to use the models here, or develop your own:

- www.nextgenscience.org/msps-wer-waves-electromagnetic-radiation

- www.nextgenscience.org/4w-waves

- www.nextgenscience.org/hs-ps4-3-waves-and-their-applications-technologies-information-transfer

- www.nextgenscience.org/4-ps4-1-waves-and-their-applications-technologies-information-transfer

If you are developing curriculum based on these standards, we encourage you to search around and see if you can invent new 3D-printable models that build on the ones in his chapter. As with Chapter 1, we hope this chapter is a starter set that will give you ideas for your own projects.

Science Fair Project Ideas

Precisely because these concepts fairly rapidly lead into some sophisticated areas, we can imagine science fair projects that involve designing and printing a variety of different types of waves to compare, contrast, and measure. It seems to us that some interesting exercises could be built around one function being the envelope or negative space of another.

More Wave Interaction Models

If you know that a complex function can be approximated by summing sine waves of different frequency and amplitude, you can experiment a bit in OpenSCAD and then print out the ones that look particularly interesting or that you would like to try comparing or fitting into one another. For rapidly variable functions, be careful of the undersampling issues mentioned earlier. The way the model is designed, you can put in more points, though they will still be 1 mm apart (but the piece will get bigger). You can scale a 3D print in MatterControl or other 3D printer slicing software if the piece gets too big for your printer.

Magnetism Explorations

As mentioned at the beginning of the chapter, the full equations that govern the wave motions of light are complex partial differential equations. Light waves are part of the broader category of electromagnetic waves. The physics of light waves and magnetism are tied together with Maxwell's equations (https://en.wikipedia.org/wiki/Maxwell's_equations), which do not lend themselves to simple solutions in OpenSCAD.

Magnetic fields have the additional representational problem that they are *directional.* The simplest example of this is a bar magnet, with its north and south poles. Typically people show magnetic field lines by sprinkling iron filings around a magnet and then noting north and south poles of the magnet. This seemed to us to be a case where adding a third dimension did not add a lot to the discussion, since a two-dimensional slice through a field with directional arrows in some ways is more information than a three-dimensional surface might be.

People who actually have to model Earth's magnetic field for navigational or other purposes resort to one of several semi-experimental models that are available. The Earth's field is "blown back" heavily by the *solar wind*—charged particles released from the Sun. The solar wind varies over time, and this variation is known as *space weather.*

The Sun's own magnetic field has some interesting interactions and also has semi-experimental models. One commonly used model is based fundamentally on an ancient mathematical construct called an Archimedes spiral. This model (https://en.wikipedia.org/wiki/Heliospheric_current_sheet) is referred to as the *Parker Spiral* after its originator.

We created some simple models that looked like magnetic fields, but after some debate we decided that the models were too simplistic and could lead readers to draw some incorrect conclusions about the more-complete mathematics. Making them "more right" would have taken us places that we felt were beyond the intended audience for this book and the desire to use simple and open source tools wherever possible. Thus we have decided not to include any magnetism models here, but we encourage advanced students and their teachers to think about what magnetic field line or potential surface models would be good for more insight. Exploring a special case or narrow application might lead to some interesting areas to explore.

Summary

This chapter developed some 3D-printable models of interacting sinusoidal waves, which are useful for modeling the physics of light, magnetism, and other phenomena. In particular, we learned about what happens when some different types of waves interact and how a light wave behaves after it passes through one or two thin slits. We learned some 3D-printing techniques (such as printing a thin object with a lot of detail on its side) and some modeling techiques (combining "negative space" models with conventional positive ones). Finally we gave various ideas for topics that could be taught with these models at grade levels from middle through graduate school.

CHAPTER 3

■ ■ ■

Gravity

No one questions the existence of gravity in everyday life. When we put something on a table (astronauts excepted), typically we expect it to stay there. Gravity is mathematically a little subtle, though, and in this chapter we look at the gravity field around the Earth and Moon, as well as that inside the triple star system that we see as the star Algol.

We also look at how moons or comets speed up or slow down in their orbits, as Johannes Kepler figured out between about 1605 and 1618. Then about 40 years later, Newton developed calculus to be able to better calculate planetary orbits. You will not need any calculus to understand this chapter, but you should be comfortable with a bit of trigonometry and some physics and astronomy. We will define terminology as we go and give some links in the main text as well as in the "Where to Learn More" section at the end.

Universal Gravitation

What is gravity? There have been many explanations throughout history, some mechanistic and involving "aether particles," and others more exotic. There was a big argument for about a century, starting with Newton and Leibnitz in the mid 1600s, about whether there was a *vis viva*, or life force, that somehow caused the effects of gravity, with or without an "aether" mediating it.

Newton thought the *vis viva* idea was nonsense, but the only place the term survives today is in his equation of planetary orbit velocity (often called the *vis viva equation*), which we model later in this chapter. People are still trying to find Grand Unified Theories that will tie gravity and other forces together, but there is not one at the moment. Einstein's general relativity (https://en.wikipedia.org/wiki/General_relativity) is the currently accepted framework for understanding gravity theoretically—and incidentally, as we were writing this book in 2016, gravity waves predicted by his explanation were observed for the first time.

In this chapter, we look at ways to visualize the gravity of planets and stars and how stars, planets, and moons orbit each other. Kepler and Newton figured a lot of it out 500 years ago, and the basics let us think about why the solar system is like it is and why it is a good idea to build bases on the moon to explore the solar system.

On Earth, gravity always points down toward the center of the Earth. Even Mt. Everest is a small enough bump on the surface of the Earth that at its peak you are not significantly farther enough from the center of the Earth to feel any difference. What happens, though, if you want to know about how the pull of gravity varies when you are in outer space? There, it is helpful to think about the *gravitational potential*. Wikipedia (https://en.wikipedia.org/wiki/Gravitational_potential) explains gravitational potential as the amount of energy needed to take a particular amount of mass from a known location to an imaginary place infinitely far away from any other masses.

Newton's Law of Universal Gravitation, which he laid out in his book *Philosophiæ Naturalis Principia Mathematica* (usually just called *Principia*) in 1687, said that the gravitational force between any two bodies is proportional to the two masses (m_1 and m_2) multiplied together and divided by the square of the distance (r) between them. The law is usually written like this:

$$Force = G\, m_1 m_2 / r^2$$

Where G is the *universal gravitational constant* (6.674×10^{-11} N–m^2/kg^2) and r is the distance between the two masses m_1 and m_2. These forces are *vectors*, which means they have a direction associated with them, so you have to be pretty careful to figure out the forces when a bunch of bodies are involved.

The gravitational potential, though, adds up all the forces and gets a single number (a *scalar*) for any particular point in space and time. This addition uses the calculus function of "integrating" the forces. The potential at any point for a particular unit of mass works out to be proportional to the sum of other masses around it divided by the distance to that mass. In other words, each mass adds to the work that needs to be done to get away from that mass in a way that gets bigger with the mass getting larger, and gets smaller as the mass gets farther away.

■ **Note**   The potential drops off as 1/distance, whereas the force drops off as 1/(square of the distance.) In calculus-speak, the potential is the integral of the forces. If that is not a language you are fluent in yet, just take our word for it: Potential = $-Gm_1(m_2/r_2 + m_3/r_3 + \ldots)$.

Gravitational Potential Wells

A planet (or moon) is a big mass, and so to get away from it you can think of "climbing out" of its *gravity well*. The good news is that the amount of energy required to climb out falls as you get farther away; the equations lead to a characteristic shape that we will see in a minute. As a side note, one of the better 2D graphics of this was done in the science cartoon *XKCD*, at https://xkcd.com/681/. A little more conventional explanation can be found at https://en.wikipedia.org/wiki/Gravity_well. Potential surfaces are by convention a bit upside-down of how you might think of them. In these models (which follow convention), the lower the surface, the more energy it takes to get out of it.

Earth-Moon System Model

With a 3D printer, we can explore this a little. Imagine a flat plane that cuts through the centers of both the Earth and Moon. Now, draw a surface above that flat plane. The height of the surface at any point is the gravitational potential (the strength of the pull of the Earth and Moon added together) at that point. However, the Moon is a lot smaller than the Earth (about one-quarter the diameter, and less dense) and so as it turns out, its contribution is much less. Therefore, potential fields around planets usually look like deep "wells."

Listing 3-1 builds on the model in Listing 1-1 to allow you to create a gravitational potential surface for the Earth-Moon system. The Earth is nearly 100 times the mass of the Moon, so to see the gravity well of the Moon at all, we can only show a small part of the well of the Earth.

■ **Caution** Listing 3-1 is a fragment; the rest of the model is the same as in Listing 1-1 from the point blocky=true. (For the models in this chapter, blocky=false). As in Chapter 2, we only show the part of the model relating to defining the function to be printed, and the number of points in each direction.

Figure 3-1 shows the resulting print. Note that the bottom of this model, however, is NOT a plane through the Earth and Moon centers - it is clipped well above the center of the bodies to allow you to see a more interesting cross-section. The small dip on the upper right is the Moon's gravity well; the bigger curve that dominates the piece is (part of) the Earth's well, which is shaped similarly to the Moon's if you could see the whole thing. Remember that the height of the curve is not representing the z dimension in space: it represents the change in energy needed to move something from a point on the plane to infinity. It is clear why it would be better to build a supply depot on the Moon if you were creating bases in deep space rather than having to lug up everything from the Earth's well.

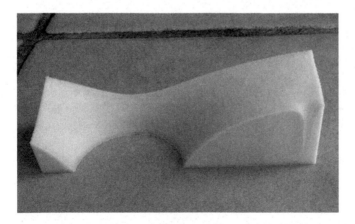

Figure 3-1. *The Earth-Moon gravity well print. The Moon's gravity well is the small notch on the upper right; the Earth's field would go down a very long way on the left side of the print. Both wells are shown here in cross-section*

■ **Caution** For all the models in this chapter, the scaling in any dimension is arbitrary as long as we are consistent. The "real" numbers are very big, so we have used scaling factors liberally to make features visible. The center of the Earth and Moon are "singularities" and would require infinite energy in this simplified example.

Listing 3-1. Earth-Moon Gravity Well

```
// OpenSCAD model to compute gravitational potential wells for earth-moon system

// Gravity potential for a unit test mass is a constant times
// the sum of mass of other bodies
// Divided by distance from test mass to those bodies
// File earthMoon.scad

  constant= 3*0.0667408 ; // km^3/kg-s^2 -- factor of 2 added to exaggerate
                          // vertical scale
  mass_earth = 5970;      // in 10^21 kg
  mass_moon =72;          // in 10^21 kg
  height_model = 50;      // z height of printed model, in mm

  //Each square in x and y is 5,000 km on a side in this model
  //Earth-moon 76.8 squares apart
  //Earth radius is 0.6 squares

  function f(x, y) = max( 0,  height_model-
            (constant*mass_earth/sqrt(x*x+(y-82.3)*(y-82.3)) +
            constant*mass_moon/sqrt(x*x+(y-5.5)*(y-5.5)) )
                          );

thick = 0;   // set to 0 for flat bottom. else mm thickness of surface
xmax = 35;   // Number of points in x direction - 1;
ymax = 120; // Number of points in y direction -1;

// If you want a rough surface (to make it more tactile) set blocky=true.
// Otherwise surface will be smoothed
blocky = false; //if true, xmax and ymax must be less than 100.
```

Algol Model

The star Algol, in the consellation Perseus, is actually composed of three stars, called Aa1, Aa2, and Ab. Their masses, relative to Aa2's mass, are 4.5, 1, and 2 respectively. As seen from Earth, Aa1 and Aa2 are at most 2.15 microarcseconds apart on the sky; Aa1 and Ab are at most 93 microarcseconds. All we need for our model are relative separations, so we will not worry about the units as long as they are consistent.

Algol was known in ancient times as the "demon star" (https://en.wikipedia.org/wiki/Algol) because it varied in brightness every few days. We know now that this is because Aa1 is far brighter than Aa2 or Ab, and the planes of their orbits line up with the Earth so that Aa1 gets eclipsed every 2.85 days by Aa2, and essentially never by Ab which orbits much farther away.

Listing 3-2 creates the gravity wells for the Algol three main stars (there are now thought to be more dark companions). Only two are visible at the scale of the model; the other one would be about 19 meters away at the scale we are using. Figure 3-2 shows this close binary pair; you can see how the two gravity potentials interact, and how there is a low-energy (higher surface) area between the two stars.

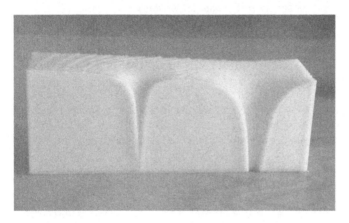

Figure 3-2. *The Algol gravity well print—a cross-section of the field from Aa2 (left) and Aa1 (right)*

Listing 3-2. Algol Gravity Well

```
// OpenSCAD model to compute gravitational potential wells of Algol system

// Gravity potential for a unit test mass is a constant times
// the sum of mass of other bodies
// Divided by distance from test mass to those bodies
// File Algol.scad

 // This is for the trinary star Algol, data from
 // http://en.wikipedia.org/wiki/Algol
```

39

```
constant= 20;      // here just a scaling factor in Z
mass_Aa1 = 4.5;    // masses relative to Aa2
mass_Aa2 = 1;
mass_Aab = 2;


//distances in milliarcseconds as seen from earth
//Aa1 to Aa2 = 2.15; Aa1 to Ab = 93.4
height_model = 40; // z height of printed model, in mm

// Each square in x and y represents is 0.2 microarcsecond
// seen from earth on a side
// The Aab star will not explicitly appear in this version
// but its influence is included for completeness

function f(x, y) = max( 0,  height_model- constant * (
                mass_Aa1 /sqrt(x*x+(y-20)*(y-20)) +
                mass_Aa2/sqrt(x*x+(y-62.2)*(y-62.2)) +
                mass_Aab/sqrt(x*x+(y-1888)*(y-1888))
                                                    ));

thick = 0;  // set to 0 for flat bottom. else mm thickness of surface
xmax =25;   // Number of points in x direction - 1;
ymax = 100; // Number of points in y direction -1;

// If you want a rough surface (to make it more tactile) set blocky=true.
// Otherwise surface will be smoothed
blocky = false; //if true, xmax and ymax must be less than 100.
```

Orbits

A gravity well is a useful concept if you want to think about the relative forces of several planets. However, planets do not hover, stationary, at a point in their star's gravity well. Instead, planets and stars orbit around one another. Technically, all the bodies in a system orbit around their mutual center of mass. Since stars are heavy and planets are (usually) of almost negligable mass, typically this means that the star (in our case, the Sun) has the center of mass of the whole system of planets inside it. In a case like Algol (discussed in the preceding section), it is more complicated.

Let us instead think about a simple case with one heavy body and one much lighter one orbiting it. Kepler figured out that in general in this situation the light body will travel in an *elliptical* orbit, with the heavy body at one *focus* of the ellipse (https://en.wikipedia.org/wiki/Ellipse). (Bodies will orbit their mutual center of mass; in this simplified case, the center of mass of the system is assumed to be at the center of the larger mass.)

Figure 3-3 shows the major features of an ellipse: the semi-major axis, usually referred to as *a* (half the longer diameter of the ellipse) and the semi-minor axis, *b*, which is half the shortest diameter. There are two foci symmetrically around the minor axis. If you draw two lines from the two foci to any point on the ellipse, the sum of the length of the lines will be equal to the length of the whole major axis (2a).

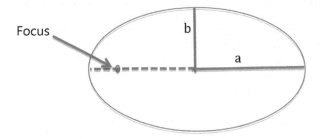

Figure 3-3. *Parts of an ellipse*

Kepler developed three laws that govern the physics of this situation, which he published between 1609 and 1619 (https://en.wikipedia.org/wiki/Kepler's_laws_ of_planetary_motion):

- *First law*: The orbit of every planet is an ellipse with the Sun at one focus.

- *Second law*: A line from a planet to the Sun sweeps out the same area during equal amounts of time (which has the collolary that planets move faster near the focus containing the Sun).

- *Third law*: The square of the time it takes a planet to go completely around the sun is proportional to the cube of the semi-major axis (*b*) of the orbit.

Isaac Newton and others built on this about 66 years later to come up with the *vis viva* equation (sometimes just called the conservation of energy equation (https://en.wikipedia.org/wiki/Vis-viva_equation):

$$v^2 = GM(2/r - 1/a)$$

where v = the orbital velocity when the lighter body is at any point r in its orbit, G is the universal gravitational constant (6.674×10^{-11} N–$m^2/kg^{2)}$, M is the mass of the heavy body, and a is the semi-major axis of the ellipse. The radius r is between the focus of the ellipse where the heavier body rests and the lighter body's position on the ellipse at any given moment. To put it another way, we assume that the heavier body is so much heavier that the center of mass of the system is assumed to be a point mass equal to the mass of the heavier body, located at one focus of the ellipse.

Halley's Comet Orbit Model

Listings 3-3 and 3-4 show a model of an elliptical orbit with the height of the surface being equal to the velocity an orbiting body would have at that point in the ellipse. In this case, it is the orbit of Halley's Comet around the Sun. Halley's Comet was the first comet to have its orbit worked out, in about 1705 by Edmund Halley (https://en.wikipedia.org/wiki/Halley's_Comet). The semi-major axis is 17.8 AU (astronomical units, the average distance from the Earth to the Sun), and it has an eccentricity, e, of 0.967. Since

$$e^2 = 1 - b^2/a^2$$

we can get the semi-minor axis, b, which turns out to be 4.54 AU. Just to make things more interesting, Halley's moves around the Sun in a retrograde orbit, going around the Sun in the opposite direction than the Earth does.

When the comet is at its closest to the Sun (the big peak in the model in Figure 3-4), we can use the vis viva equation with $r = 0.6$ AU (and the fact that 1 AU = 1.487×10^8 km). If you sort out the units (be careful of the units in G) in more convenient units for this problem, converting Newtons (N) to its component units of kg - m/s² and simplifying, $G = 6.674 \times 10^{-20}$ km²/kg – s^2. Use 1.989×10^{30} kg for the mass of the Sun.

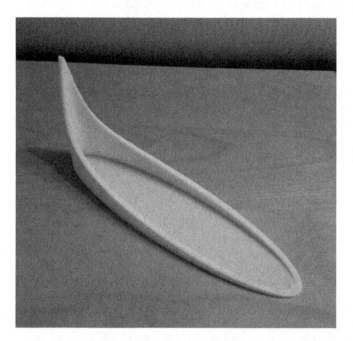

Figure 3-4. *Halley's Comet orbit model. Dots (partially buried in the model wall since the eccentricity is so extreme) are foci, height is instantaneous orbital velocity. The Sun is at the focus at the base of the high-velocity part of the orbit*

You wind up with the velocity of Halley's Comet at *periapsis* (closest point to the Sun) of about 55 km/s. This is remarkably close to the real value (usually quoted, just as we did, as "about 55 km/s"). The real value varies some due to the effects of other planets (notably Jupiter and Saturn).

Listing 3-3. Modeling the Orbital Speed of Halley's Comet

```
// OpenSCAD model to compute the velocity of a body in a Keplerian two-body orbit

// Version to visualize speed of Halley's Comet around the sun.
// Note that Halley is retrograde, so the speed relative to the earth
// adds about 30 km/s to the number you will calculate here
// File HalleysComet.scad

AU_to_mm = 4; // scaling factor for x and y axes
slice_angle = 1;
a = 17.8*AU_to_mm;  // semi-major axis - in AU times a scaling factor to fit
b = 4.54*AU_to_mm;  // semi-minor axis - in AU times a scaling factor to fit
z_scale_factor = 70;
// scale of z axis is arbitrary
// because z is velocity, but
// x, y are physical distance

//use the OpenSCAD hull() function to create
for(theta_hull = [0:slice_angle:359.99]) hull()
    for(theta = [theta_hull, theta_hull + slice_angle],
    // Use the parametric equations to generate an ellipse with one focus at (0,0)
        x = a * (cos(theta)) + sqrt(a*a-b*b), y = b * sin(theta),
        r = sqrt(x*x + y*y),

    // Use the vis-viva equation to calculte the height to represent
    // instantaneous velocity
        h = z_scale_factor* sqrt((2/r - 1/a)))

    // then generate a rectangular solid aligned with the tangent of the
    // curve of the ellipse
    // so that the hull operation makes the smoothest possible surface
                    translate([x, y, h/2])
                        rotate(theta)
                cube([3, .0001, h], center = true);

//generate the base and dots for the two foci
translate([sqrt(a*a-b*b), 0, 0]) scale([1, b/a, 1]) cylinder(r = a, h = 1);
translate([0,0,1])sphere(r = 1, h = 50);
translate([2*sqrt(a*a-b*b),0,1]) sphere(r =1);
```

To test out the equation for the Earth's speed around the Sun, we can for purposes of calculation here assume that the Earth's orbit is close to circular ($r = a = 1.487 \times 10^8$ km—we give the actual numbers later in Table 3-1). If you put those into the vis viva equation, terms drop out and you get out about 30 kilometers per second. If you use the same radius of the orbit and say that the earth goes around the Sun in an orbit that is about 2π times the same radius in a year ($365 \times 24 \times 60 \times 60$ seconds), gratifyingly we get the same number of about 30 km per second. (The official number is 29.8).

Table 3-1. *Parameters Needed to Create an Inner Solar System Model*

Planet	a (AU)	b (AU)	e	AU_to_mm	Z_scale_factor
Mercury	0.387098	0.378826	0.205630	50	100
Venus	0.728213	0.728196	0.00677323	50	100
Earth	1.000003	1.000002	0.00167112	50	100

By the way, if you want to think about what would happen if Halley's Comet hit the Earth, the bottom line is that no one would be around to talk about it afterwards. At $r = 1$ AU (where the comet's orbit crosses Earth's orbit), the comet is going about 42 km/s the other way from the Earth, so it would be a head-on collision. The numbers work out to about 72 km/s if you just add them, but Halley's orbit is a little bit inclined to that of Earth so it would be a little less. Wikipedia says the relative velocity in 1985 was about 70 km/s (but, of course, Halley's crossed the 1 AU point when the Earth was somewhere else).

Inner Solar System Model

Next, we will try printing the orbits of Mercury, Venus, and Earth to the same scale. We will use the model in Listing 3-3, but with values as shown in Table 3-1. You can see how the three of them came out relative to each other in Figure 3-5 (side by side) and 3-6 (nested). We do not assume a circular orbit here, because the model does not handle that case. It does, however, handle very small eccentricities.

Figure 3-5. *Earth, Venus, and Mercury orbit models side by side. Dark spot on the Earth model marks the focus (here the two foci more or less are collapsed into the center point since Earth and Venus orbits are very close to circular)*

Figure 3-6. *As in Figure 3-5, but nested lined up on approximately on the focus (as if the Sun were at the focus of each orbit). Height of each point on the orbit is the instantaneous velocity*

The nested version is not completely accurate because each orbit has a 1 mm thick base plus a 1 mm bump showing where the foci are, creating a net offset of 2 mm for each orbit you stack. But you can get a good qualitative idea of how these orbits relate to each other. As you would expect, the closer a planet is to the Sun, the faster it is going around in its orbit. You might want to play with the model to create ways to make them stack more accurately if you are using them for a science fair project.

The stacked models in Figure 3-6 show this quite nicely, with Mercury's orbital eccentricity visible. Since the bases of the models are only 1 mm thick, they are translucent. We marked the focus with a permanent marker so that we could look through the model bottoms against a light and line them up. Earth and Venus were so nearly circular that the two foci were both more or less on the centerpoint. If two or more had been elliptical, you would need to look up how the orbits phased.

Printing Tips

The models in this chapter are relatively straightforward to print. The gravity well models were printed in the orientation in which they appear in Figures 3-1 and 3-2. They have solid bases and are pretty sturdy, particularly compared to the models in the last chapter. The models pictured in this chapter were printed in PLA on a Deezmaker Bukito, using MatterControl software and CuraEngine slicing software. Figure 3-7 shows the Mercury and Earth orbit models being printed. (We wanted the Venus orbit in between to be a contrasting color, so we skipped Venus for this print grouping.)

Figure 3-7. *Mercury and Earth orbital velocity models on the printer*

However, very elliptical orbits (like Halley's Comet) are a little challenging in that the tallest parts are going to tend to get a bit too pointy to print completely cleanly. The model shown in Figure 3-4 was printed along with a cooling tower, 0.1 mm layers, a bit lower print speed than we would normally use. We also raised the minimum layer time (to slow down the printer on the pointy bit). These are all things that you can do in an open source software system like MatterControl.

The other thing we did was to make the afore-mentioned *cooling tower*, a separate feature that prints on the bed along with the model but is intended to be discarded afterwards. To add a cooling tower, add a cylinder or other tall skinny object (as a separate object) that is as tall as the tallest part of the orbit model. This is a stalling tactic—the printer has to take time to make the tower and that allows more time for each layer of the model to cool (this also has the advantage that there is not a hot nozzle in contact with the plastic you are trying to cool). You can play a bit with the *x/y* scaling factor AU_to_mm and the *z* scaling `z_scale_factor` to work out these issues. Be careful to add a brim to the print, though, so the tower is not knocked over too easily.

To add a cooling tower to the model in Listing 3-3, add these lines to the end:

```
hmax = z_scale_factor* sqrt((2/(a-sqrt(a*a-b*b)) - 1/a));
translate ([a/2,b+12,0]) cylinder (r=8, h=hmax);
```

Figure 3-8 shows the model on the printer with the cooling tower. You can see that there is no free lunch, and now we get a bit of stringing on the model where it is near the tower which was not the case when we printed the model without the tower. There are other parameters you can adjust for this, like lowering the temperature a bit and slowing the print down still more. You may need to experiment a bit with your own printer, within the limits of the modifications to settings that your printer allows. Figure 3-9 shows how using a cooling tower creates a much crisper cusp on the orbit.

Figure 3-8. *The Halley's Comet orbit model with its cooling tower*

Figure 3-9. *The Halley's Comet orbit model peak printed without a cooling tower (L) and with one (R)*

THINKING ABOUT THESE MODELS: LEARNING LIKE A MAKER

We continue to be surprised at how deeply we have to go into the physics background to develop what initially seemed to be a simple model. We have found ourselves reprising Kepler and Newton's lines of reasoning as we tried to represent these concepts. Many planetariums have "gravity well" models, but it requires a little thought to consider what representations will actually give some insight for the interactions of two or more gravity wells. Scaling is fundamentally arbitrary, and for the first model in the chapter we had to experiment some to come up with a scale where the Moon's effect was visible while retaining some of the features of the Earth's potential field.

For the model of Algol's system, we had to abandon actually showing the third star in the triple star system because to do so would have made it impossible to see the separation between the two closer ones. Detail insets do not really work with 3D printing, unless you simply make models at two different scales or elect to use logarithmic scales in some of the dimensions. But if the point is to make a model that reflects physical reality, using nonlinear scaling can feel like defeating the point.

For the orbital velocity model, we wrestled with too much choice. Should we try to show some sort of surface of all possible models? Should we pick one orbit, or try to interleave many? In the end, we went for simplicity, but you may want to experiment with ways to use these representations to do your own walk through the history of calculus and physics. We found ourselves wanting to do the experiment of printing a few planets at the same scale and looking at how the velocity distribution varied among the inner three planets. You could do a perspective graph in 2D, but it might not occur to you until you were playing with the models!

Where to Learn More

There are many places you can take these explorations. We cited Wikipedia background articles as we went along, but you can kick it up a notch by looking up data about other solar systems to make a gravity-potential model or make a model of other planetary orbits, or orbits of moons of planets. You might look into the history of astronomy and in particular the history of the study of gravity. It seems hard to believe now, but gravity as a force without some medium to transmit it was very controversial for at least a century. You might think about how the models we made in this chapter might have looked different over the last two millennia.

The Kepler space mission (named after the Kepler we cited a lot in this chapter) has been discovering a lot of *exoplanets*—planets around other stars. You can try making yourself some models of these new solar systems with data from http://kepler.nasa.gov/Mission/discoveries/.

Teacher Tips

Much of the material in this chapter lends itself to supporting undergraduate physics and/or calculus, since some of the early development of calculus was in fact intended to solve these problems. The special cases (two-body problems) we show here are good for building intuition, but need to be extended carefully to more general cases where these simple models may not apply (see the note that follows). As we noted in the previous section, the vis viva controversy and the deep issues of standards of proof and limits of observational technology at the time could be used in a discussion of how science evolves.

For our K-12 colleagues, we looked at the Next Generation Science Standards to see what topics might benefit from the models and ideas in this chapter. Generally, they fall under MS. Space Systems (www.nextgenscience.org/msess-ss-space-systems) and Earth's Place in the Universe, particularly "MS-ESS1-2 2 develop and use a model to describe the role of gravity in the motions within galaxies and the solar system" (www.nextgenscience.org/ms-ess1-2-earths-place-universe).

NASA also has some teacher resources in this sphere. Take a look at the Kepler spacecraft's education resources, which can be found at http://kepler.nasa.gov/education/EducationandPublicOutreachProjects/.

Science Fair Project Ideas

There are many ways you can extend some of the ideas in this chapter. Some basic ones would be to apply some of the equations to more detailed models than the simples ones here. For example, if you allow for the fact that the orbits of most of the planets in the solar system are slightly elliptical, what is their orbital velocity at a given point in the orbit? How would the orbit of a comet appear?

More sophisticated projects might involve trying to develop a model of the gravity well of one of the stars that has an eclipsing companion, as Algol does, and then observe for yourself the actual stars eclipsing, and also use the orbit equation to determine what the period should be if you can look up the orbital parameters. The general principles for Algol are described in this 2014 *Scientific American* article, but you can deduce the general principles (www.skyandtelescope.com/astronomy-blogs/behold-algol-star-secret/).

■ **Note**   Be a little careful applying the orbital velocity equation, as it only applies in the form given for two-body systems—that is, one planet and one star, ignoring all other effects. In our solar system the effects of the other planets are small compared to the Sun, but in star systems with three or more stars (like the Algol system) the orbits of the stars are about their common center of mass, not about one of the stars. It can take a stellar system a while to settle down into stable orbits, and young stars can be in *trapezia*—systems of stars that are not yet in stable orbits around their mutual center of mass.

You might also think about how you would model escape velocity and other types of orbit, like a *hyperbolic* orbit—where something moving very fast just flies close to a gravitating body and then ricochets back out into space again. You could also think about what it might be like to be on an planet that had a very elliptical orbit—could life evolve there? What would it be like to live there?

Summary

In this chapter, we learned about gravity and experimented with models of the gravitational potential field around stars and planets. Next we looked at some ways to model the orbital velocity of planets, moons, and stars in their (elliptical) orbits. These models are mostly special cases of general physics phenomena that require calculus techniques to analyze, so the models need to be taken with a grain of salt. Still, they can be used as starting points for explorations in understanding our own solar system and the dynamics of other systems of distant stars as well.

CHAPTER 4

■ ■ ■

Airfoils

Flying is so much a part of our lives that it is hard to remember that the ability to fly a heavier-than-air vehicle is barely more than a century old. The Wright brothers (Figure 4-1) succeeded where many others failed largely because of their extremely systematic approach to the problems of flight, and their recognition that the biggest problem to overcome was the control of their craft.

Figure 4-1. Wilbur Wright gliding to the right, attributed to either Orville or Wilbur Wright, 1902. Original on a glass negative, from the Library of Congress' collection. Image in the public domain in the United States because of its publication before January 1, 1923. Retrieved from www.loc.gov/pictures/resource/ppprs.00604/

■ **Tip**   Orville and Wilbur Wright's pragmatic, low-budget approach will be very familiar to today's makers. David McCollough's *The Wright Brothers* (Simon and Schuster, 2015) explores their approach, which could give you some ideas on the type of experiments you might want to do. Or you might just find it inspiring to see how two people with limited resources solved problems that defeated large, well-funded traditional institutions.

A critical part of an airplane's design is its wings. The cross-section of a wing is called an *airfoil* (or *aerofoil*, if you hail from a place that speaks British English). A modern airplane also usually has parts of the wing that move to help control the airplane, making the wing a pretty complex robotic device, not to mention the rest of the plane.

The design of a modern airline wing is a complex undertaking, occupying huge teams of people for years. However, we can get a lot of insight by looking back to a time when things were simpler and a lot more experimentally based than they are now.

This chapter looks at some historic airfoils and gives you an opportunity to 3D print them. The intent here is not to make something fly-able as much as to make something that will be a good base for experiments in a classroom or for a science fair project. If you are an aviation history buff, you will be able to create wings of some World War II–era airplanes.

■ **Note**   The math behind these models is more sophisticated than that behind other models in this book. In one place a basic calculus idea is used; if you have not yet had calculus, we try to explain what is going on in words, but generally speaking you can just skip that part and use the models without really understanding the math entirely. We use pseudocode for most of the equations—a mix of normal algebra symbols, but with * to show multiplication and some variables that in textbooks will just be single letters or a single letter with a subscript spelled out here instead.

How Airfoils Work

In the Wright brothers' day (around 1903) and for some time thereafter, airplane wings were made of fabric and strategic wood stiffeners. Every plane was an experiment, and each wing was laid up and tweaked individually. By the 1930s, engineers started to want to have some standards to work with, and our models will use some basic standards that were first defined about that time: the NACA airfoils.

Flight Forces: Lift, Drag, Gravity, and Thrust

How airplanes fly is complicated in detail. However, we can simplify it down to some basics here. Four forces are acting on an airplane. First is *gravity* pulling downward. Next there's *thrust* (the plane's engines) pushing it through the air. Then pushing the plane up is *lift*, and slowing it down (acting against the thrust) is *drag*. Lift and drag are closely related and affected strongly by the geometry of the aircraft.

When a plane is airborne (Figure 4-2) in stable flight, these four forces are in balance and the airplane moves ahead at a constant speed. If thrust is greater than drag, the aircraft accelerates; if there is more lift than gravity, the plane can climb. The wings have a cross-section (the airfoil) which is usually not symmetrical. In most airfoils, the top is curved more than the bottom. This makes air on top move faster and be at a lower pressure than air forced across the bottom, since air moving faster is less dense than air moving slower. This is not quite the whole story, though.

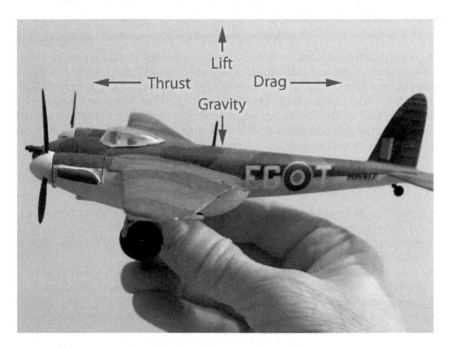

Figure 4-2. *Forces on an aircraft, shown on a model of a World War II British Royal Air Force fighter-bomber, the deHavilland Mosquito—one of the last bombers made of wood. (Model courtesy of Stephen Unwin.)*

You will also notice that wings tend to be rounded at the front (the *leading edge*) and pointy at the back (the *trailing edge*). A pointy edge means that air cannot circulate around the wing and get up into the lower pressure area above; instead, the flow around the wing throws off big *vortices* (swirling masses of air) that otherwise would have wanted to curl up around the wing. This is called the *Kutta Condition* (www.grc.nasa.gov/www/K-12/airplane/lifteq.html).

The equation for lift is *Lift* = 0.5 * CL * ρ * v^2 * A. Here's what the symbols mean: the density of the air in which the aircraft is traveling is the Greek letter ρ (pronounced "rho"). v^2 is the square of its velocity. A is the *planform area* of the wing (the area of the wing as seen from above). Finally, C_L is a fudge factor called the *lift coefficient* (https://en.wikipedia.org/wiki/Lift_coefficient) which depends on the geometry of the wing and some factors about how the plane is flying, and is usually measured experimentally.

■ **Example**   At sea level, if a plane is going 100 miles an hour at takeoff (about 45 m/s), air density is 1.23 kg/m³, wing area is around 100 square meters, and lift coefficient is about 1, then we get about 124 kN, or 27,000 pounds-force, of lift. The lift coefficient usually varies a lot with the angle the plane's nose is holding relative to the horizontal, called *angle of attack* (more on this in a later section).

Drag is the resistive force that holds back the airplane as it flies through the air. Drag is the same equation as lift, with a different coefficient (C_D instead of C_L). There is a list of of some values of drag coefficient for different shapes at https://en.wikipedia.org/wiki/Drag_coefficient. So that your plane can fly a long way on a reasonable amount of fuel, you need to have a big lift coefficient and a small drag coefficient. In practice they are closely related, and airplane designers have to work to get one as big as possible and push the other down. The ratio of lift to drag is a common performance metric for aircraft.

Chord, Camber, and Thickness

The Wright brothers built on work by others, notably George Cayley (1773–1857), who has been generally credited with defining some of the key features of working wings. If you look at a bird, you see that the wing has a lot of structure and is not just a flat plate tilted to the wind somehow.

Over time, people have developed conventions for ways to describe a wing. There are a lot of subtle ones, but we will just talk about a few of the easiest-to-understand ones in this chapter (and give you some suggestions about where to learn more at the end). Figure 4-3 is a diagram of the parts of an airfoil. The straight-line distance from the leading edge to the trailing one is called the *chord*.

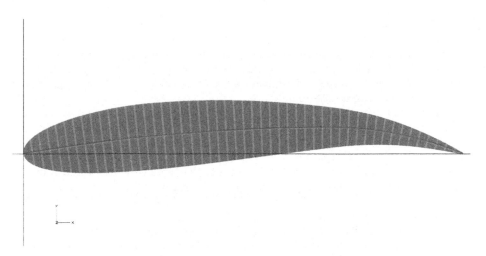

Figure 4-3. *Airfoil (NACA 6715). The red middle line is the camber line*

Wings usually are curved a bit from front to back. The line that describes this curve is called the *camber line*. The *thickness* of the airfoil is how thick it is, typically measured at the point of maximum thickness or maximum camber.

Camber, thickness, and the location of maximum camber and maximum thickness are typically given relative to the chord (as a percentage of, or in tenths of, the chord.) Or to put it another way, the numbers are figured out for a chord that is 1 unit long, and you would then scale everything accordingly. In Figure 4-3, the chord is the straight (*x*-axis) line distance from leading to trailing edge. The red line right through the middle is the camber line. The short grey lines from the upper to the lower surface, perpendicular to the camber line, represent the thickness of the airfoil at any given point along the camber line.

■ **Note**   If you have had some calculus, you can read about the Kutta-Jukowski theorem (https://en.wikipedia.org/wiki/Kutta%E2%80%93Joukowski_theorem) to understand a bit better how the phenomenon called *circulation* creates lift on a wing. For our purposes here, it is enough to think about a wing throwing off air partially downward to create a lift force. A big, heavy aircraft has so much energy in the vortices it leaves in its wake that aircraft have to be separated by miles to allow the vortices to dissipate. There is also a good interactive discussion of all these topics in the *NASA Glenn Beginner's Guide to Aeronautics* at www.grc.nasa.gov/ www/K-12/airplane/.

NACA Airfoils

After World War I ended, it was clear that some design rules about how to make a good wing were needed to take the next steps in aviation. The Aerodynamic Research Institute of Göttingen, in Germany, did one of the first systematic studies of wings, called *Joukowsky Profiles*, from 1923–1927.

Meanwhile, in the United States, the National Advisory Committee on Aeronautics (NACA) was formed in 1915 to coordinate aeronautics research. (In 1958, it was closed down and merged into NASA.) In 1932, according to a NASA history chronology (www.hq.nasa.gov/office/pao/History/Timeline/1930-34.html), a first set of *NACA airfoils* was published, which are thought to have been inspired to some degree by the German ones. Over the next few years *wind tunnel* tests (see sidebar) were performed on some of the more promising airfoils. More sets were developed over time and have since been published and put in the public domain.

Fundamentally, the NACA profiles gave an equation for the camber line relative to the chord and another one for how thick the airfoil should be at any point along the chord. These equations were experimentally developed, and a lot of the theory about why these were good airfoils came much later.

WIND TUNNELS

A *wind tunnel* is, in its most basic form, a box with a fan on one end and an opening on the other which allows an engineer to flow air over a model in a controlled way. A model is held on a *sting* (which can just be a stick), and the different forces on it are measured somehow. Or sometimes a tunnel will just have a way to mix a little smoke in with the flow so that users can watch what the smoke does when it interacts with the vehicle design. The wing models we show you how to make in this chapter are designed to allow you to explore how a wing works, or just to appreciate some early wing designs as works of engineering art.

In the "Science Fair Projects" suggestions at the end of this chapter, we have some links to project sites that talk about how you might build a small student wind tunnel for students to learn about basic aerodynamics.

The NACA Four-Digit Series

The first set of NACA airfoil profiles are called the *four-digit profiles*, because each profile is defined with four numbers, like NACA 2412 (a classic airfoil that is still used in some general-aviation aircraft today). The digits of the airfoil NACA *abcd* are interpreted as follows:

- *First digit (a)*: the maximum distance the camber profile goes above the chord (in what we are calling the y direction), as a *percentage of the chord*. You multiply this number by 0.01 times the chord to get the actual distance. If the chord was 1 meter long, for a 2412 airfoil the maximum camber distance from the chord would be 2 times 0.01 times 1 meter, or 0.02 meters (2 cm).

- *Second digit (b)*: the location along the chord, in what we are calling the *x* direction, starting at the leading edge where the maximum camber occurs as a *tenth* (not a percentage) of the chord. You multiply this number by 0.1 times the chord to get the location. For our 1 meter chord wing and a 2412 airfoil, this means this location would be 0.4 times 1 meter from the leading edge, or 40 cm from the leading edge.

- *Third and fourth digit (cd)*: The maximum thickness above and below the chord, as a percentage of the chord. There is an equation to plug this number into to get the thickness at any given point along the chord. The maximum thickness in our example would be 12% of 1 meter, or 120 cm on *either side* of the camber line, and is measured perpendicular to the camber line (see Figure 4-3).

To summarize our example (NACA 2412, $a = 2$, $b = 4$, $cd = 12$) has a thickness that is 12% of the chord; has a camber that is 2% of the chord at its maximum point; and that maximum happens 40% of the chord away from the leading edge of the wing (Figure 4-4).

Figure 4-4. NACA 2412 model, as created by the model in Listing 4-1

In the section later in this chapter, "Thinking About These Models: Learning Like a Maker," we talk about how we went all the way back to a 1935 report to wade through inconsistent naming conventions for these parameters (some people use *mpxx*, some *pmxx*, some other things). We also shuffled the equations around a little to make them work better with OpenSCAD. Here we walk through them from first principles. If you look them up elsewhere, you will find the equations a little different. We found in many places online that they were simply wrong, so use online sources like people's class notes or Wikipedia with care.

Later on, other NACA airfoil series were developed that had more complicated profiles. The early ones were intended to be rules of thumb that could be used as guides in the pre-computer days. Now wings are very complicated things, but you can learn a lot by going back to those simpler times and re-creating some of these early experiments.

NACA Four-Digit Profiles in OpenSCAD

The NACA four-digit airfoil model is made up of two curves: a *camber line* that defines the curve of the centerline of the airfoil, and a *function* that defines how thick the airfoil is on either side of this curve. Confusingly, *camber* is the distance from the chord to the camber line.

The Camber Line

The *camber line* is derived from two parabolas, each of which has a maximum at the point of maximum *camber* (Figure 4-5). Everything in what follows is computed for a wing with a unit chord; everything will then be scaled to that proportionately. The *x* axis is along the chord. The equations of the parabolas for the camber line are as follows:

- For *x* less than or equal to *b*:

  $ycamber = (a/b^2)(2bx - x^2)$

- For *x* greater than or equal to *b*:

  $ycamber = ((a/(1 - b)^2)(1 - 2b + 2bx - x^2)$.

  Notice that when x = b, then either one results in ycamber = a.

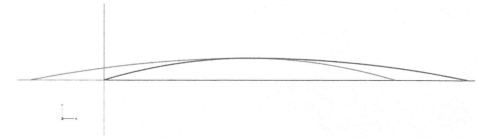

Figure 4-5. *The two parabolas making up the camber line. The red line is the halves of the two parabolas that are used to create the camber line, while the grey line is the unused portion of each parabola. The maximum is at x = b, y = a, if the chord is equal to 1*

The Thickness Equation

The camber line is just an abstract, infinitely thin line. The *thickness equation* tells us how much the airfoil extends at any point on either side perpendicular to the camber line. The equation for thickness that follows is what you might think of as half the thickness of the wing; it is how far away the wing surface is from the camber line, toward the upper or lower surface.

Some airfoils have different top and bottom thickness profiles, which complicates deriving the camber line. The NACA four-digit ones use the same equation for both, and thus the camber line could be written as a (relatively) simple equation as well. For the four-digit airfoils the maximum thickness as a percentage of the chord is the last two digits (*cd*) of the NACA airfoil:

$$thickness(x) = (cd/20)(0.2969 * sqrt(x) - 0.1260 * x - 0.3516 * x^2 + 0.2843 * x^3 - 0.1015 * x^4).$$

However, this is the thickness *perpendicular to* the camber line, and assuming that the chord is 1 unit long. To get it in terms of x and y, we want to figure out what direction is perpendicular to the line. An easy way to do this (if you have had calculus) is to take the derivative (the slope) of the tangent line. (See the "Learning Like a Maker" section for references for these equations, which were in somewhat different form in the 1935 reference.)

The equations of the slope of the camber line, $d(ycamber)/dx$, are as follows:

- For x less than or equal to b:

  $$d(ycamber)/dx = (2a/b^2)(b - x)$$

- For x greater than or equal to b:

  $$d(ycamber)/dx = ((2a/(1 - b)^2) * (b - x)$$

If you have not had calculus yet, what we are doing here is picking a point on the camber line and figuring out what the slope of a line that is tangent to the curve of the camber line is at that point. (Isaac Newton needed to solve similar problems and invented calculus to do it.) Then we use that tangent line to figure out how to get the thickness (which is defined in a direction perpendicular to the camber line) at that same point. If you like, you can think if it as transforming the thickness into a coordinate system that is sliding along the camber line.

To do that coordinate transformation, we first define an angle *theta* to be the angle whose tangent is $d(ycamber)/dx$. Then the equations we get for the airfoil surface (camber line plus thickness component perpendicular) are as follows:

$$theta = arctan(((2a/(1 - b)^2) * (b - x))$$

$$x(lower) = x + sin(theta) * thickness(x)$$

$$y(lower) = ycamber - cos(theta) * thickness(x)$$

$$x(upper) = x - sin(theta) * thickness(x)$$

$$y(upper) = ycamber + cos(theta) * thickness(x)$$

In our OpenSCAD model (Listing 4-1), we do not actually calculate the x and y coordinates of each point on the upper and lower surface. Instead, we just use OpenSCAD's built-in rotate() function to rotate a shape centered on the camber line so that its minimum and maximum points fall on the upper and lower surface lines. Ideally, these shapes would simply be line segments with a length determined by the thickness function. You can see these ideal lines in the grey lines perpendicular to the camber line in Figure 4-3.

However, because OpenSCAD does not have a concept of lines with no area or volume, we simulated these lines with very thin rhomboids (Figure 4-6), which become infinitely thin where they meet the top and bottom surface lines. We created these using a "circle" with four sides with circle($fn = 4) and scaling this "square circle" in the x and y directions. circle($fn = 4) is a shorter way of producing the same thing we would get by creating a square measuring two units corner-to-corner and rotating it, which you would do in OpenSCAD with rotate(45) square(sqrt(2), center = true). Note that the rhomboids in Figure 4-6 are thicker and fewer than the ones actually used to make the wing profile.

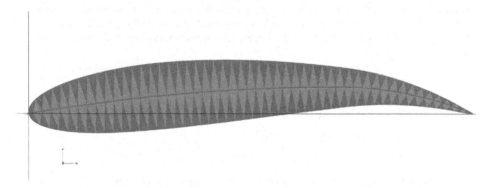

Figure 4-6. *The geometry of rhombuses which are bisected by the tangent to the camber line. Airfoil is NACA 6715*

We then use the convex hull fuction hull() to fill in the space between each of these rhomboids in order to create the profile of our wing. All this results, in our first pass, in an airfoil that has a NACA four-digit profile (and is a *flat wing*—not swept back. Listing 4-1 gives the model for this basic wing, which also has the capability of using *sweep* and *taper* (defined in the next section).

Listing 4-1. The Model for a NACA Profile Wing

```
//OpenSCAD model to print out a NACA airfoil
// Formulation of NACA airfoil mathematics based on equations in
// NACA Report 460, "The Characteristics of 78 Related Airfoil Sections
// From Tests in the Variable-Density Wind Tunnel" (1935) by
// E.N. Jacobs, K.E. Ward and R.M. Pinkerton.
// File airfoil.scad
```

```
NACA = 2412;   // Airfoil to print - this is broken into abcd parameters below
chord = 60;    // Chord length, mm
length = 120;  // wing length, mm

taper = 1; // taper ratio: ratio of chord at root to chord at tip
sweep = 0; // if wing is swept , sweep angle in degrees ; if 0, no sweep

if((taper == 1 || taper == 0) && sweep != 0)
echo("ERROR: Sweep without taper is not currently supported!");

step = 1/500;

$fs = .5;
$fa = 2;

airfoil();

//Extract the wing parameters from the NACA number
// and insert them in array p[]

function parameters(NACA) = [(NACA - NACA % 1000) / 100000,
    (NACA % 1000 - NACA % 100) / 1000, NACA % 100];

//Develop the camber line,
function camber(x, p) = (
    (x < p[1]) ?
        p[0]/pow(p[1], 2)
    :
        p[0]/pow(1 - p[1], 2)
    ) * -pow(x - p[1], 2) + p[0];
//mirror camber
function camber_(x, p) = (
    (x < p[1]) ?
        p[0]/pow(p[1], 2) * (2 * p[1] * x - pow(x, 2))
    :
        (p[0]/pow(1 - p[1], 2)
    ) * ((1 - 2 * p[1]) + 2 * p[1] * x - pow(x, 2)));

//Determine the thickness
function thickness(x, p) = (p[2] / 20) * (0.29690 * sqrt(x) - 0.12600 * x -
    0.35160 * pow(x, 2) + 0.28430 * pow(x, 3) - 0.10150 * pow(x, 4));

 //Find instantaneous angle of slope of the camber curve, theta,
 // so that the thickness component can be
 //computed perpendicular to the camber line

function theta(x, p) =
    atan((p[0]/pow(((x < p[1]) ? p[1] : 1 - p[1]), 2) * (2 * p[1] - 2 * x)));
```

61

```
//Draw create the full airfoil from the cross-section by
//extruding the cross-section

module airfoil(
    p = parameters(NACA), chord = chord, length = length, taper = taper,
    sweep = sweep
) {
    translate([-chord / 2 * 0 + length * taper * tan(sweep) + chord / 4, 0, 0])
        linear_extrude(length, center = false, scale = 1/taper)
            translate([-length * taper * tan(sweep) - chord/4, 0, 0])
                airfoil_cross_section(p, chord);
}

//Create the cross-section by hulling a series of rhomboids bisected by a tangent
// to the camber line with a height equal to half the wing thickness

module airfoil_cross_section(p, chord)
    for(x_ = [step / 10:step:1 - step])
        hull() for(x = [x_, x_ + step]) {
            translate([x * chord, camber(x, p) * chord, 0]) rotate(theta(x, p))
                scale([chord * step / 10, thickness(x, p) * chord])
                circle($fn = 4);
            translate([x * chord, camber_(x, p) * chord, 0]) rotate(theta(x, p))
                scale([chord * step / 2, chord * step / 2]) #%circle(r = 2,
                $fn = 4);
        }
//End of model
```

Other Aerodynamic Parameters

Modern wings are rarely straight across with the same airfoil cross-section all the way along the wing. Here are some other things that affect how a wing works (and how it appears). The models in this chapter can handle the following two variables, in addition to their airfoil profiles:

- *Sweep*: If you look at a modern jet aircraft, the wings sweep back at an angle, rather than having a leading edge that is straight across. This became important once jet aircraft were introduced and planes were going very fast. Jet aircraft now cruise near the speed of sound; right at the speed of sound, a plane creates shock waves that are experienced on the ground as sonic booms and on the plane in a variety of ways. A swept wing allows the plane to fly closer to the speed of sound than it would if it had a straight wing.

- *Taper*: Tapered wings get thinner as they get farther from the fuselage (but maintain the same airfoil cross-section, as implemented here). The model in this chapter requires that swept wings be tapered. You might want to play with the two variables and see how the models change.

- *Angle of attack*: Airplanes tilt up steeply as they are climbing away from the ground both because they are trying to get away from the ground quickly, but also because (to a point) a higher angle relative to the flow generates more lift (see previous section). The angle of the chord line to the horizontal direction of flight is called angle of attack. Typically drag also increases with angle of attack, so this is one of the many things to trade off in aircraft design. (We talk about this when we get to the model in Listing 4-2.)

The current model does not support some other wing design features such as *dihedral*. If the wings bend upward from the root to the tip, we say that the wings "have dihedral" or that the dihedral angle is greater than zero. The angle is defined from a line perpendicular to the chord. Dihedral has implications for aircraft stability.

Classic Airplanes Using NACA Airfoils

The NACA models were developed a little before World War II. All the airplanes flying in those days were what we would now consider to be low speed. The NACA airfoils were used heavily in World War II airplanes on all sides of the conflict. *The Incomplete Guide to Airfoil Usage,* at http://m-selig.ae.illinois.edu/ads/aircraft.html, has many examples. The same group's home page at http://m-selig.ae.illinois.edu/ads.html has links to other aircraft modeling tools and sites.

You will see on the site that many airplanes used one airfoil design at the root of the wing (where it connects to the fuselage) and another at the tip. For example, according to the *Incomplete Guide*, the workhorse early prop-driven airliner, the DC-3, used NACA 2215 at the root and 4412 at the tip. Many Cessnas have used the common 2412 airfoil.

If you are a fan of British aviation history, the *Incomplete Guide* notes that the World War II Supermarine Spitfire used two NACA profiles in its wings (2213 at its root, 2209.4 at its tip, where the decimal point means 09.4% maximum thickness). The Spitfire was the classic Royal Air Force (RAF) interceptor during the Battle of Britain. Figure 4-7 is a kit created in the 1960s by the child of a WWII RAF officer.

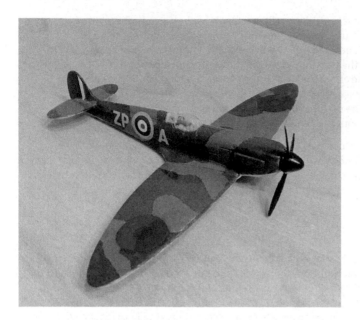

Figure 4-7. *WWII Supermarine Spitfire model (courtesy of Stephen Unwin)*

We have not created the capability to replicate the exact details of any given actual wing (the model requires that you have one NACA profile for the whole wing). Rather, our intent is that you can pretend to be the designer of an historic vehicle and play around with changing its basic profile. In short, how might you have designed an airplane during World War II? Or for a low-speed application today? Or to understand why different birds have the wing shapes they do? It is all yours to explore.

Using the 3D-Printed Airfoil Models

The basic OpenSCAD model in Listing 4-1 will print one wing. If it is not symmetric (if it is swept, for example) you will need to use MatterControl (see Appendix A) or your equivalent 3D-printer software to mirror the wing if you want two to make yourself a whole airplane to study.

If you want to study the aerodynamics of a wing, Listing 4-2 creates two wings and a test stand (called a *sting*) that will allow it to stand in a wind tunnel or other place that you make observations or measurements. We are also including a version of the model (Listing 4-2) that includes a sting with a ratched mechanism that allows you to vary the angle of attack in a range that you set. The next section talks about simple ways to measure lift.

■ **Caution** The sting model is intended to allow for some basic classroom experiments in changing angle of attack and measuring the resulting lift. It is not very aerodynamic and introduces a lot of drag, and we have not talked about measuring drag. If you are interested in measuring anything other than lift, we suggest going back to the OpenSCAD model and adding your own attachments for more sophisticated instruments. Since this is an open source model, see Appendix A for links to add your creation, if you would like, to the community (and to see what others might have added since the book was published).

Listing 4-2. OpenSCAD Model for a Pair of Wings Plus a Sting (Test Stand)

```
// OpenSCAD model to print out a pair of NACA airfoils
// (to make a complete wing)
// Plus a support that can be used for measuring lift
// Formulation of NACA airfoil mathematics based on equations in
// NACA Report 460, "The Characteristics of 78 Related Airfoil Sections
// From Tests in the Variable-Density Wind Tunnel" (1935)
// by E.N. Jacobs, K.E. Ward and R.M. Pinkerton.
// File airfoilStand.scad

NACA = 2412;  // Airfoil to print - this is broken into abcd parameters below
chord = 30;   // Chord length, mm
length = 120; // wing length

taper = 1; // taper ratio: ratio of chord at root to chord at tip
sweep = 0; // if wing is swept , sweep angle in degrees ; if 0, no sweep

sting_size = 20;    // sting cross section in mm
sting_length = 100; // sting vertical and horizonal bar length, in mm

sting_angle = [0:5:25]; //range of angle of attack possible

nest = false; // Attempt to nest parts for printing, may not fit with certain options

if((taper == 1 || taper == 0) && sweep != 0) echo("ERROR: Sweep without
taper is not currently supported!");

step = 1/500;

$fs = .5;
$fa = 2;

airfoil_with_sting();
%mirror([0, 0, 1]) airfoil_with_sting();
%translate([chord * 1.5 + sting_size/4, -sting_length, -sting_size/2]) base();
```

```
if(nest) {
    translate([chord * 1.5 - sting_size / 2 - 20, -45, 0]) base();
    translate([chord * 1.5 - sting_size/2, sting_size, 0]) mirror([1, 0, 0])
    airfoil_with_sting();
} else {
    translate([0, 50, 0]) base();
    translate([-5, 0, 0]) mirror([1, 0, 0]) airfoil_with_sting();
}

//Extract the wing parameters from the NACA number
// and insert them in array p[]
function parameters(NACA) = [(NACA - NACA % 1000) / 100000,
    (NACA % 1000 - NACA % 100) / 1000, NACA % 100];

//Develop the camber line
function camber(x, p) = (
    (x < p[1]) ?
        p[0]/pow(p[1], 2)
    :
        p[0]/pow(1 - p[1], 2)
) * -pow(x - p[1], 2) + p[0];

function camber_(x, p) = (
    (x < p[1]) ?
        p[0]/pow(p[1], 2) * (2 * p[1] * x - pow(x, 2))
    :
        (p[0]/pow(1 - p[1], 2)
) * ((1 - 2 * p[1]) + 2 * p[1] * x - pow(x, 2)));

//Determine the thickness
function thickness(x, p) = (p[2] / 20) * (0.29690 * sqrt(x) - 0.12600 * x
    -0.35160 * pow(x, 2) + 0.28430 * pow(x, 3) - 0.10150 * pow(x, 4));

//Find instantaneous angle of slope of the camber curve, theta,
// so that the thickness component can be
//computed perpendicular to the camber line
function theta(x, p) = atan((p[0]/pow(((x < p[1]) ? p[1] : 1 - p[1]), 2) *
(2 * p[1] - 2 * x)));

//Draw create the full airfoil from the cross-section by extruding the
// cross-section
module airfoil(
    p = parameters(NACA), chord = chord, length = length, taper = taper,
    sweep = sweep
) {
```

```
        translate([-chord / 2 * 0 + length * taper * tan(sweep) + chord / 4, 0, 0])
            linear_extrude(length, center = false, scale = 1/taper)
                translate([-length * taper * tan(sweep) - chord/4, 0, 0])
                    airfoil_cross_section(p, chord);
}


// Create the cross-section by hulling a series of rhomboids
// centered on the camber line
// with a height equal to half the wing thickness

module airfoil_cross_section(p, chord) for(x_ = [step / 10:step:1 - step])
    hull() for(x = [x_, x_ + step]) {
        translate([x * chord, camber(x, p) * chord, 0]) rotate(theta(x))
            scale([chord * step / 10, thickness(x, p) * chord]) circle($fn = 4);
        translate([x * chord, camber_(x, p) * chord, 0]) rotate(theta(x, p))
            scale([chord * step / 2, chord * step / 2]) %circle($fn = 4);
}


*translate([chord / 4, 0, 0]) rotate([0, sweep, 0]) %cube(100);

module airfoil_with_sting() translate([0, 0, 0]) union() {
    airfoil();
    hull() {
        translate([chord * parameters(NACA)[1], chord * parameters(NACA)[0], 0])
            intersection() {
                sphere(r = chord * thickness(parameters(NACA)[1],
                    parameters(NACA)));
                    translate([0, 0, chord/2]) cube(chord, center = true);
            }
            translate([chord * 1.5 - sting_size/4, chord *
            parameters(NACA)[0], 0])
                intersection() {
                    rotate([0, -90, 0]) rotate_extrude() rotate(-90)
                    intersection() {
                        airfoil_cross_section(parameters(0040), sting_size);
                        square(sting_size);
                    }
                    translate([0, 0, sting_size]) cube(sting_size * 2,
                    center = true);
                }
        }
    difference() {
        translate([chord * 1.5 - sting_size/4, chord * parameters(NACA)[0], 0])
            rotate([90, 0, 0]) linear_extrude(sting_length) intersection() {
                airfoil_cross_section(parameters(0040), sting_size);
                square(sting_size);
            }
```

```
            translate([chord * 1.5 + sting_size/4, -sting_length, -1])
                cylinder(r = sting_size/2 - 3, h = sting_size);
    }
    translate([chord * 1.5 + sting_size/4, -sting_length, 0]) intersection() {
        rotate([-90, 0, 0]) rotate_extrude(convexity = 10) hull() {
            difference() {
                circle(r = sting_size / 2 + 1);
                translate([0, -50, 0]) square(100);
            }
            translate([-50, 0, 0]) circle(r = 1);
        }
        linear_extrude(sting_size / 4, convexity = 10) difference() {
            hull() {
                circle(r = sting_size / 2);
                translate([-50, 0, 0]) circle(r = 1);
            }
            circle(r = sting_size/2 - 4, $fn = 8);
        }
    }
}

module base() {
    difference() {
        linear_extrude(sting_size, convexity = 10) difference() {
            intersection() {
                circle(50 + 5);
                translate([-100 + sting_size, 100 - sting_size, 0])
                    square(200, center = true);
                rotate(-max([for(i = sting_angle) i]))
                    translate([-100 + sting_size, -100 + 5, 0]) square(200,
                    center = true);
            }
            circle(50 - 2);
            for(i = sting_angle) rotate(-i) hull() {
                circle(r = sting_size / 2 + 3);
                translate([-50, 0, 0]) circle(r = 1.1);
            }
        }
        for(i = sting_angle) rotate(-i) hull() for(j = [1, -1])
            translate([0, 0, sting_size + 5 * j - 3]) linear_extrude(1)
            offset(1.5 * j)
                hull() {
                    circle(r = sting_size / 2 + 3);
                    translate([-50, 0, 0]) circle(r = 1.1);
            }
    }
}
```

```
    linear_extrude(sting_size / 4) difference() {
        intersection() {
            circle(50 + 5);
            translate([-100 + sting_size, 100 - sting_size, 0])
                square(200, center = true);
            rotate(-max([for(i = sting_angle) i]))
                translate([-100 + sting_size, -100 + 5, 0])
                    square(200, center = true);
        }
    }
    difference() {
        intersection() {
            linear_extrude(73) difference() {
                intersection() {
                    circle(50 + 5);
                    translate([-100 + sting_size, 7 - sting_size, 0])
                        square([200, 14], center = true);
                    rotate(-max([for(i = sting_angle) i]))
                        translate([-100 + sting_size, -100 + 5, 0])
                            square(200, center = true);
                }
            }
            translate([-100, 0, 80]) rotate([-130, 0, 0]) cube(200);
        }
        intersection() {
            linear_extrude(100) difference() {
                intersection() {
                    circle(50 + 5 - 3);
                    translate([-100 + sting_size, 7 - sting_size + 3, 0])
                        square([200, 14], center = true);
                    rotate(-max([for(i = sting_angle) i]))
                        translate([-100 + sting_size, -100 + 5, 0])
                            square([200 - 6, 200], center = true);
                }
            }
            translate([-100, 4, 80]) rotate([-130, 0, 0]) cube(200);
        }
    }
    hull() {
        cylinder(r = (sting_size/2 - 4) * cos(180 / 8) - .2, h = sting_size - 2);
        cylinder(r = (sting_size/2 - 4) * cos(180 / 8) - .2 - 1, h = sting_size);
    }
}
//End model
```

Measuring Lift

We saw earlier in this chapter that $Lift = 0.5 * C_L * \rho * v^2 * A$, where ρ is the density of air (about 1.23 kg per cubic meter). The lift coefficient, C_L, will vary with angle of attack but will be around 1 or 2 (see the 1935 report referenced in the "Thinking Like a Maker" section that follows). The model in Listing 4-2 creates a pair of wings, a sting, and a stand that you can weigh down (with coins, for instance).

You also need to attach the two wings to each other, say with blue tape (as we show here) or by gluing. The base will let you set an angle of attack range. In the example, it goes from 0 to 25 degrees in 5-degree increments.

Then, if you put the whole thing on a sensitive scale (like an electronic postal scale, or a scale you have in your school lab) you will get a setup that looks like the one in Figure 4-8. This model used a NACA 2412 airfoil with a chord 60 mm long, a taper of 2, and a wing length of 80 mm (times 2, for the pair).

Figure 4-8. *Using the output of the model in Listing 4-2 to measure lift*

■ **Tip**   To get the area of a tapered wing, you have to figure out the area of a trapezoid with the sides being the root chord and tip chord. To do that, you average the two chords and multiply by the wingspan. In the case of our example, we would get

Area = 0.5 * (*tip chord + root chord*) * *wingspan*. In our example here,

Area = 0.5 * (60 mm + 30 mm) * 80 mm * 2 *wings* = 0.0072 *square meters.*

For more planforms, see www.grc.nasa.gov/www/k-12/airplane/area.html.

If the airflow is about 9 miles per hour (about 4 meters per second), then the lift should be around 0.5 * 1 * 1.23 * 4 * 4 * 0.0072 = 0.0709 Newtons, or has the ability to lift about 7 grams if you prefer to think that way, for a drag coefficient equal to 1.

■ **Tip**   For more ideas on simple ways to measure lift, see the slides "Wind Tunnel Experiments for Grades 8–12, " available at www.grc.nasa.gov/WWW/k-12/airplane/topics.htm.

If you zero out the scale when the fan is off, you should get a negative number for the weight of the sting plus the airfoil when you turn it on. That number is the lift (with a fair number of sources of error). The model (Figure 4-9) allows you to play with the angle of attack, and of course you can print different profiles. You will need to find some way of measuring how fast the flow coming out of the fan is, and its direction—you can make, buy, or borrow a *cup anemometer* as a simple instrument (a search will reveal both plans to make and places to purchase one). You can take a small piece of string and hold it in front of the wing to see if you are in an area of the fan outflow that has smooth airflow. We guesstimated the flow out of the fan by dropping a small scrap of tissue and seeing how long it took to go a few meters, but this is really too error-prone to use closer than a factor of two or so, since the flow mixes very quickly with the ambient still air.

Figure 4-9. *Closeup of the angle of attack ratchet on the support*

In our experiment here, an angle of attack of zero gave us enough lift to raise about 10 grams; of 15 degrees, about 13; and of 25 degrees, about 8 grams. The 1935 paper seems to show that a clean 2412 wing should have a lift coefficient about 0.2 at 0 degrees angle of attack; about 1.3 at 15 degrees; and at around 25 degrees or so it should stall and drop off precipitously. Given the many variables (like the effects of the test stand and the placement in the fan's not-particularly-even flow) this is more or less reasonable. We encourage you to work out ways to make this far more accurate!

Household fans often have dead spots. You may need to play around a bit to get good results—staying a couple feet away from the fan helps, but not too far, since the flow will be too diffuse. To do this right, you need to create a wind tunnel, the device that controls air around a test airplane; see the "Building a Student Wind Tunnel" resources at the end of the chapter.

■ **Note** These models are not meant to be flying models. They will barely lift their own weight at reasonable speeds. They are meant to be sturdy enough to stand up to some experimentation and analysis, rather than being as light as possible. Your 3D printer software will give you a weight estimate for the wing (which in the case of the Listing 4-2 models will include the sting and the base).

Printing Suggestions

These models are meant to be as easy as possible to print, given that the geometry is fairly complicated. Print them with the chord side down, as the models were designed. You should not need to use support, but you probably want to use a brim or raft so that the model sticks to the platform. For the STL output by Listing 4-2, you may need to move the pieces around to fit your platform, or print it in more than one print. You will want to make sure that you have printer settings that allow brim or raft to be removed cleanly, though, because any remaining pieces will interfere with assembly of the sting mechanism. Figure 4-10 shows how the model appeared on the 3D-printer platform.

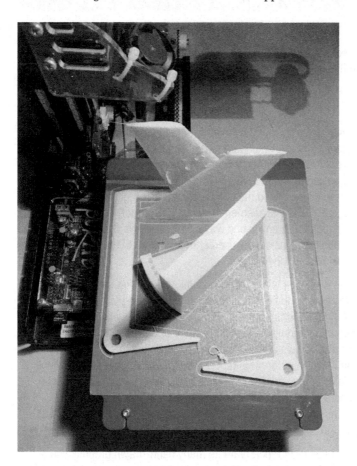

Figure 4-10. *The layout of the models as printed*

■ **Caution** Do not scale these models in your 3D printing program; use the scaling parameters in the models in OpenSCAD and generate a new STL. There are issues of tolerances and some complex interactions that may break if you just scale without taking account of these issues.

THINKING ABOUT THESE MODELS: LEARNING LIKE A MAKER

When we started this chapter we thought we would be done in a couple of hours. We knew there were equations for the NACA airfoils, and we thought we would use techniques similar to those in we used in Chapter 1 to create the top and bottom as 3D surfaces.

No such luck.

The NACA airfoils are interesting in that they were created to make hand calculation (in the 1930s) as simple as possible, and were purely empirically based. They were also extensively cited, but inconsistently. Over time, authors seem to have lost some of the assumptions underlying the original model, or just appeared to make transcription errors. Some authors used the letter p for the first digit, and m for the second; somewhere in the 1970s this seemed to reverse. (To avoid getting a lot of letters from people who found references one way or the other, we changed here to an *abcd* convention.) Authors inconsistently used either the ratio of the thickness to the chord, or the dimensioned number.

We decided to go all the way back to the oldest possible description of the NACA series and to look at the physics there. Fortunately, all these old reports are available for free from the NASA Tech Reports Service (http://ntrs.nasa.gov). We started digging and discovered that the report everyone seemed to cite as a first place the airfoils were described in detail was NACA Report 460, published in 1935 by E.N. Jacobs, K.E. Ward, and R.M. Pinkerton. This report, *The Characteristics of 78 Related Airfoil Sections from Tests in the Variable-Density Wind Tunnel*, is an amazing period piece. Two of the advisors listed in the front matter were Charles Lindbergh and Orville Wright! Pages 4 and 5 of the report have very clear drawings that we used as the basis of the OpenSCAD model.

If you look in the back of the 1935 report (with its many hand-drawn graphs), you can see wind tunnel data that might be a good place for you to begin designing a classroom demonstration or a great science fair project.

Where to Learn More

There is a tremendous amount of information out there about airfoils; the challenge for this chapter has been to curate a set of interesting explorations that would be accessible for a wide range of student levels. In this section, we suggest some sensible bigger projects for you to take on if just informally playing with these airfoils is not enough. Another good general site on the topic, in addition to ones given so far, is http://airfoiltools.com, which has a variety of interesting calculators and plotting tools.

NASA Glenn Research Center also has an exhaustive site with many good ideas. The main index is at www.grc.nasa.gov/WWW/K-12/airplane/bgt.html, and many presentations available for teachers are indexed at www.grc.nasa.gov/WWW/K-12/airplane/topics.htm.

You can take projects about airfoils in several directions. As a first thought, you can look at it as the history of aviation and the study of the development of aviation from 1903 through the 1930s and beyond. Or you can treat this as a basic physics exercise to see how changing some of these basic parameters like camber and thickness changes the lift and drag of the wing.

Building a Student Wind Tunnel

To actually test out the wings in a quantitative way, you will need to make yourself some sort of wind tunnel. We have not tried this ourselves, but with that caveat we will note that this project seems plausible, although probably best suited for a group, rather than individual, project: www.sciencebuddies.org/science-fair-projects/wind-tunnel-toc.shtml. If you wanted to build a tunnel purely to visualize the flow around the wing (versus trying to measure lift and drag), this Instructable has a simpler build: www.instructables.com/id/DIY-Wind-Tunnel-20-Project-Paperclip/.

Visualizing Flow

To learn more about ways to visualize what the air flowing over wings is doing, try searching on "flow visualization." There is also a classic book you might hunt down: *An Album of Fluid Motion,* by Milton Van Dyke (Parabolic Press, 1982), which is just an entire book of pictures of flow in various test conditions.

Scaling a Model

If you are going to seriously try to model a real system (like a bird or an airplane) with a wind tunnel model that is a lot smaller than the original, you will need to match the *Reynolds number (Re)* of your model and the real system to get accurate results. The Reynolds number is a ratio of the kinetic energy in a system to the effects of *viscosity.* Viscosity is how "sticky" a fluid is—maple syrup is pretty viscous, but air less so. (Engineers do not draw distinctions between liquids and gases here—it's all "fluids" to us.)

High *Re* flow could be found in a fast-flowing water stream; low *Re* is exemplified by molasses coming out of a jar. The two extremes behave quite differently. The equation for Reynolds number is usually written: $Re = \rho \, v \, L / \mu$.

Where ρ is still the density of the air (or fluid) around the wing, v is the velocity, L is a characteristic length of the thing you are testing (like the chord or the wingspan), and μ is the dynamic viscosity of the air or other fluid.

If you are modeling something big with a 1/10th scale model, to have the Reynolds number of your model be the same as the real thing you need to run your test with ten times higher velocity or ten times denser or more viscous flow (or a combination that works out to that). For air at the surface of the earth at 15 degrees Centigrade, the density and viscosity are, respectively, $\rho = 1.23$ kg/m³ and $\mu = 1.78$ x 10^{-5} kg/m-s; for water, $\rho = 999$ kg/m³; and $\mu = 115.4$ x 10^{-5} kg/m-s (from A.M. Kuethe and C-Y Chow, *Foundations of Aerodyamics* 3rd Edition (Wiley, 1976).

Using flowing water as a test fluid is thus the same as air at the same velocity around an object about 12 times bigger. *Water tunnels* have been developed to exploit this, but obviously this is pretty challenging and messy.

Teacher Tips

The science of flight is usually not encountered in depth until undergraduate-level science courses, since to get very far into the analysis you really need to have some calculus. That said, the empirical study of the forces on a wing might fit well under the NGSS standards (MS-PS-2, www.nextgenscience.org/msps2-motion-stability-forces-interactions) and Energy standards (MS-PS-3, www.nextgenscience.org/msps3-energy).

That said, there are many topics that could be covered purely to build intuition. We have suggested many possible experiments in this chapter; some might lend themselves to labs at almost any level. In particular, working to refine how accurate the model is will be a good long-term project for any number of students.

Science Fair Project Ideas

A wind tunnel, even the small ones described in the "Where to Learn More" section, is probably physically too big to bring to most science fairs. However, if a school or class builds one, testing a series of models to find their lift and drag might be an interesting project.

You might also see which airfoils could approximate a bird's wing and try to think about how to model how well a bird "should" fly.

But if all that sounds too complicated, you can always create a few airfoils and just test them qualitatively in front of a box fan. Consider ways to make simple ways to measure lift and drag using weights to balance the forces. Or perhaps create some wing cross-sections to see which ones might match various bird wings. Or, for that matter, you can just drag them through a bathtub and see if you can feel any difference.

Summary

In this chapter, we talked about airfoils and offered a simple model that was used in the 1930s to learn more about how wings work. We discovered that the mathematics behind flight are complex, but that there are some simplified models, like the NACA airfoils, that can help build intuition (and that are still in use today). We looked at how we might use those models today to learn about flight, and perhaps to help understand birds or other flying creatures.

CHAPTER 5

■ ■ ■

Simple Machines

Simple machines are devices that change the amount, or *magnitude*, of force or the direction of a force being exerted on something. The standard list of simple machines (at least as far as school science standards define them) are the *pulley, screw, wheel and axle, inclined plane, wedge,* and *lever*. Most of these are very old—the wheel's origin is lost in antiquity, Archimedes knew about the lever, screw, and pulley about 2,300 years ago, and the rest were used to build the pyramids (but not included in Archimedes's list of machines).

The physics behind simple machines, though, was not clarified in some cases till the late 1700s. There is a good history of these technologies on the Wikipedia page https://en.wikipedia.org/wiki/Simple_machine. The force-lessening effect that these machines exploit is called *mechanical advantage*. Often it is manifested by moving an object over a distance more slowly but with less force than one would without the intervention of a machine—for example, pushing something up a ramp (inclined plane) versus lifting it straight up.

Physics Background

Most of the things we normally think of as *machines* are combinations of these basic simple machines. Using more than one simple machine creates a *compound machine*. For example, a wheelbarrow is a combination of a lever (the handle) and two wheels on an axle (at least, for the version we show in a later figure).

Typically simple machine discussions focus on unpowered machines—ones that rely on human (or animal) power that is then converted into mechanical energy of some sort, with or without amplification, based on the geometries of the machine.

In this chapter, we have created basic versions of the six simple machines in OpenSCAD with the intent that you can 3D print them individually to use as demonstrations. The OpenSCAD model for each is designed so that you can vary critical dimensions to build intuition about how the effects of each machine changes as a result.

Each machine may have some particular caveats about scaling, which we talk about as we introduce them. You will also want to experiment with combining simple machines into compound ones. We give one example of a combination after we introduce all six machines.

Friction and *flexing* of the machine lower their efficiency to a greater or lesser degree, and you should bear that in mind if your experiments do not achieve the mechanical advantage that your calculations might indicate.

The Machines

We developed OpenSCAD models for each of the six simple machines, and in the next few sections we go over the process for 3D printing them one at a time. You can also use them as building blocks to create more complex devices. But be sure to look at the notes about combining the machines later in this chapter for some things to think about, particularly if you want to scale them or to print several of them at once in varying orientations.

■ **Note**   We give some examples of each machine and a bit about its history as we go. If you are interested in the history of basic inventions like these in general, the book *Cathedral, Forge and Waterwheel* by Frances and Joseph Gies (HarperCollins, 1994) has in-depth discussions of the paths that some machines took. The ancient Greeks in about the third century BC thought about five of the simple machines (which did not include the inclined plane). The Egyptians used the inclined plane and lever (but not the wheel) about 4,600 years ago to create the Great Pyramid of Giza. There are Wikipedia articles about each of the simple machines that list more history as well.

Inclined Plane and Wedge

Inclined planes and wedges are pretty similar, and the model we created makes one of each at the same time. We talk about each machine first, and then go over the model and the models it creates.

Inclined Plane

The inclined plane creates mechanical advantage by allowing you to move something upward at an angle so that you can exert a lower force than you would if you had to raise it vertically or more steeply. Alternatively, you can convert gravitational potential energy into kinetic energy, as in downhill skiing. The cost may be that you need to move the object for a longer period of time or over a longer distance, or both. A ramp is an inclined plane, as is a flight of stairs. Think about how much easier it is to walk up a trail with switchbacks versus going straight up a mountain.

The mechanical advantage of an inclined plane is the horizontal distance it spans divided by its maximum height; the longer and shallower the ramp, in other words, the greater the advantage. A ramp that is 10 feet long and rises 2 feet has a mechanical advantage of 5 to 1. The cost is that the user needs to traverse a longer distance to go up the same vertical rise. Wikipedia's article (https://en.wikipedia.org/wiki/Inclined_plane) has some very lucid explanations.

Wedge

A wedge is closely related to the inclined plane. A wedge either can force apart two objects, or can hold something in place. An axe or a knife are wedges, as is the end of a crowbar (the rest of it being a lever), as are the "headstones" at the top of parking spaces that keep someone from pulling too far forward into a space.

Frictional force is important with a wedge, and although the mechanical advantage here is also length divided by maximum width, how well the wedge stays put or forces in without bending matters a lot. Figure 5-1 shows the two "machines" as they were printed. Both have a 30-degree angle, but the inclined plane is a right triangle, and the wedge is an isoceles triangle to make it easier to push into place between things.

Figure 5-1. *Inclined plane (L) and wedge (R), printed on their sides*

Wedge and Inclined Plane Models

The model in Listing 5-1 generates both an inclined plane and a wedge (described in the next section) since one is an adaptation of the other. The model has three parameters you can change, listed in Table 5-1. We recommend that you do not make the wedge or plane a lot smaller than about half the default size shown here, since then the numbers may not print well.

Listing 5-1. Wedge and Inclined Plane

```
// A model which creates both a wedge and an inclined plane
// File wedgePlane.scad

length = 100;   // length of longest side in mm
angle = 30;     // angle of the plane or wedge, in degrees
width = 50;     // length of one side of the triangle (height inclined plane,
                // max width wedge)

wedge(length, width, angle);
translate([0, -length * tan(angle) - 5, 0]) inclined_plane(length, width, angle);

module wedge(length = 100, width = 50, angle = 30, isoceles = true)
difference() {
    linear_extrude(width, convexity = 5) intersection() {
        square([length, length * tan(angle)]);
        rotate(angle - 90) square([length * sin(angle), length / cos(angle)]);
        if(isoceles) rotate(angle / 2 - 90)
            translate([-length * sin(angle / 2), 0, 0])
                square([length * sin(angle / 2) * 2, length * cos(angle / 2)]);
    }
    if(isoceles) translate([length, 0, width / 2])
        rotate([0, 90, angle / 2])
            translate([0, length * sin(angle / 2), 0])
                linear_extrude(height = 1, center = true, convexity = 5)
                    text(str(angle, "°"), size = min(width / 3, length *
sin(angle / 2)), halign = "center", valign = "center");
    else translate([length, length * tan(angle) / 2, width / 2])
        rotate([0, 90, 0])
            linear_extrude(height = 1, center = true, convexity = 5)
                text(str(angle, "°"), size = min(width / 3, length *
tan(angle) / 2), halign = "center", valign = "center");
}

module inclined_plane(length = 100, width = 50, angle = 30)
    wedge(length = length, width = width, angle = angle, isoceles = false);
```

Table 5-1. *Wedge and Inclined Plane Variables*

Variable	Default Value and Units	Meaning
length	100 mm	Length of longest side
angle	30 degrees	Angle of the plane and wedge
width	50 mm	Length of one side of the triangle (height of the inclined plane, max width of the wedge)

■ **Note**   The model in Listing 5-1 3D prints both a wedge and inclined plane—it is not a choice based on a variable. You always get both.

Lever

A lever is one of the most elegant of the simple machines. All you need is a long beam of some sort that can pivot around a supporting point (the *fulcrum*). Levers are often put into three categories.

Class 1 Levers

A *class 1* lever has the fulcrum somewhere toward the center of the beam. Applying force downward on one side results in an upward force on the other. If the beam's length on either side of the fulcrum is equal, there is no mechanical advantage. However, if one side is longer than the other, the mechanical advantage is the ratio of the lengths of the two sides. In principle there is no limit to how long a lever can be, but it needs to be mechanically strong enough to lift the load without snapping or breaking the fulcrum support. Figure 5-2 shows a class 1 lever on the printer, and Figure 5-3 with a load.

Figure 5-2. *Class 1 lever on the printer*

In Figure 5-3 the person's finger is showing where to apply force. Note that the Class 1 lever has two indentations so that you can hang a weight at both ends if you want to. However, since the lever itself has finite (and unequal) mass on either side of the pivot and the pivot swings very freely, it is difficult to use this as a balance. It is best used to get a qualitative feel for the force to move an object attached to one end for a few different configurations.

Figure 5-3. *Class 1 lever*

You might want to print out several different positions for the fulcrum and feel the difference in force for the same weight applied to the end of each.

Class 2 and 3 Levers

Other relationships apply for the other two classes of lever. Class 2 levers have a fulcrum on one end, and a load is toward the center of the beam. An upward force on the end opposite the fulcrum will pivot the load.

A class 3 lever has the weight to be moved at one end and the fulcrum at the other. Force is applied at the marked spot partway along to pull up the load. Figure 5-4 shows a class 2 lever, and Figure 5-5, a class 3. Class 2 levers always have mechanical advantage greater than 1:1, and class 3 always worse than 1:1. Note that you have to hold the class 3 lever down at the fulcrum, too, in this design.

Figure 5-4. *Class 2 lever*

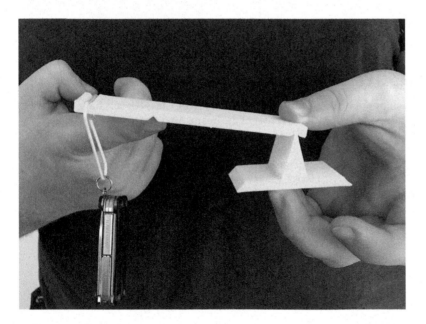

Figure 5-5. *Class 3 lever*

The model in Listing 5-2 creates a lever and fulcrum. Table 5-2 describes the variables you can change to try out different configurations.

■ **Caution** The lever STL file is laid out as two pieces—the lever and the fulcrum—oriented as they would be when used with each other. For small-bed 3D printers, you might need to use MatterControl's separation function in Edit mode to split the pair into two STLs that you can move around. See Appendix A's section on MatterControl software.

Listing 5-2. Lever Model

```
// A model which creates all three classes of lever
// Percentage on either side of fulcrum printed on lever
// Designed to be printed on its side
// File lever.scad

lever = [70, 30]; //Length of the on either side of the fulcrum (class 1) or
                  // load or resistance application point (class 2/3)
class = 3; //class of lever
fulcrum_height = 30; //height of point of fulcrum, in mm
width = 30;  //width in mm

linear_extrude(width, convexity = 5) difference() {
    intersection() {
        square(fulcrum_height * 2, center = true);
        rotate(-135) square(fulcrum_height * sqrt(2));
    }
    difference() {
        square(fulcrum_height * 2 - 10, center = true);
        intersection_for(a = [1, -1])
            rotate(-135 + a * (45 - 15)) square(fulcrum_height * sqrt(2));
    }
}

difference() {
    linear_extrude(width, convexity = 5) difference() {
        translate([-5 - ((class == 1) ? lever[1] : 0), 0, 0])
            square([10 + lever[0] + lever[1], 5]);
        translate([0, 2.5, 0]) rotate(-135) square(5);
        translate([lever[0], 2.5, 0]) rotate(((class == 3) ? -135 : 45))
        square(5);
        translate([((class == 1) ? -lever[1] : lever[0] + lever[1]), 2.5, 0])
            rotate(((class == 2) ? -135 : 45)) square(5);
    }
```

```
        translate([lever[0] / 2, 5, width / 2])
            rotate([90, 0, 180])
                linear_extrude(height = 1, center = true, convexity = 5)
                text(str(lever[0]), size = min(width / 3, lever[0] / 3),
                    halign = "center", valign = "center");
    translate([(class == 1) ? -lever[1] / 2 : lever[0] + lever[1] / 2, 5,
    width / 2])
            rotate([90, 0, 180])
                linear_extrude(height = 1, center = true, convexity = 5)
                text(str(lever[1]), size = min(width / 3, lever[1] / 3),
                    halign = "center", valign = "center");
}
```

Table 5-2. *Lever Variables*

Variable	Default Value and Units	Meaning
lever[a,b]	lever[70,30] (mm)	Length of the lever on either side of fulcrum (class 1) or load/resistance application point (class 2 or 3)
class	1, 2, or 3	Type of lever
width	30 (mm)	Width of lever and fulcrum

Screw

We usually think of a screw as something that holds things together. More generally, though, turning a screw takes rotational motion and changes it into linear motion along the screw's axis. 3D printers often use a screw to drive one or more of their axes.

Screws used as fasteners (for example, machine screws with nuts) are designed to use mechanical advantage to convert rotational force into tensile and compressive forces to produce friction to hold things in place.

The mechanical advantage of a screw is proportional to how far apart the threads are (the *pitch);* the closer they are, the higher the advantage. However, screws are usually far off the ideal for most practical purposes because there is so much friction on a screw embedded in a material. Wikipedia has a very good brief explanation at https://en.wikipedia.org/wiki/Screw_%28simple_machine%29.

Our example of this simple machine is a model of a vise (the real thing in Figure 5-6, and our model in Figure 5-7). The model prints in just two parts: the upper crossbar and the rest of the model. The knob to turn the screw is printed in place (captive). This is an example of a model that is not really possible to create any other way than by 3D printing it (if it is being fabricated in one piece, anyway).

Figure 5-6. *A vise*

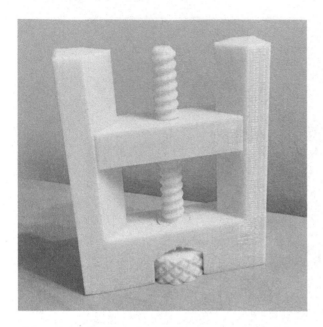

Figure 5-7. *Vise (screw) model*

The printed vise of course is not strong enough to use for anything that will exert a lot of force, but it will be interesting to play with and get some intuition about the relationships between the things you can vary for this model. The variables you can tweak are listed in Table 5-3; the model for the vise model is in Listing 5-3.

Table 5-3. *Vise Model Variables*

Variable	Default Value and Units	Meaning
fn	12	Sides used to approximate circles (raise for smoother print)
tolerance	0.4 mm	Tolerance between moving parts—raise if parts are binding, lower (a tiny bit) if too loose
pitch	4	Screw pitch (see narrative)

The vise model should be printed in the same orientation shown in Figure 5-7 (vertically), with the crossbar piece flat on the platform next to it. If you screw the crossbar all the way to the bottom, you will discover that there is a slight gap. This is intentional, to orient the layers of the crossbar to allow smoother movement by preventing the layers from catching on one another.

Listing 5-3. Vise Model

```
// A model which creates an example of a screw
// In the form of a model of a vise
//Prints in two pieces, with the bigger piece printing vertically
// (screw knob on bottom)
// File vise.scad

fn = 12; // Fragment number- OpenSCAD polygon sides parameter
tolerance = .4; // Spacing parameter (make bigger if parts stick together)
pitch = 4; // Screw pitch

function profile(d = 10, pitch = 2) = [[0, d/2 - pitch/4], [pitch * .3, d/2],
    [pitch * .5, d/2], [pitch * .8, d/2 - pitch/4], [pitch, d/2 - pitch/4]];
    //a function that generates the points for the thread profile

intersection() {
    rawthread(profile = profile(10, pitch), turns = 100/pitch,
internal = false, fn = fn);
    hull() for(i = [0, 80]) translate([0, 0, i]) cylinder(r = 20, r2 = 3,
    h = 20);
}

// Create captive knob
intersection() {
    rotate_extrude(convexity = 5, $fn = 24) difference() {
        square([13.5, 25]);
        hull() for(i = [20, 22]) translate([5, i, 0]) rotate(-45)
        square(20);
        translate([6, 13, 0]) square(8);
        translate([7, 20, 0]) square(20);
    }
    union() {
        translate([0, 0, 70]) cube(100, center = true);
        for(i = [0:30:90-1], j = [0:3:20-1]) translate([0, 0, j])
        rotate(i + j * 45 / 3) cylinder(r = 15, r2 = 12.25, h = 3, $fn = 4);
            for(i = [0:30:90-1], j = [0:3:20-1]) translate([0, 0, j])
        rotate(i + j * 45 / 3 + 45) cylinder(r = 15, r1 = 12.25, h = 3,
        $fn = 4);
    }
}

// Create separate slider next
translate([0, 50, 0]) difference() {
    linear_extrude(15, convexity = 5) square([80, 20], center = true);
    rotate([0, 2, 0]) {
        linear_extrude(100, center = true, convexity = 5) offset(tolerance)
```

```
    for(i = [0, 1]) mirror([i, 0, 0]) translate([20, 0, 0]) rotate(-45)
    square(100);
        translate([0, 0, -25]) rawthread(profile = profile(10 + tolerance *
        2, pitch),
            turns = 100/pitch, internal = true, fn = fn);
    }
}

// Create rails for slider
linear_extrude(100, convexity = 5) intersection() {
    square([80, 20], center = true);
    for(i = [0, 1]) mirror([i, 0, 0]) translate([20, 0, 0]) rotate(-45)
    square(100);
}

// Create the base
difference() {
    linear_extrude(25, convexity = 5) square([80, 20], center = true);
    rotate_extrude(convexity = 5, $fn = 24) difference() {
        offset(tolerance + (1/cos(180/24) - 1) * 20) difference() {
            square([14, 25]);
            difference() {
                hull() for(i = [20 + tolerance*0, 22 - tolerance*0])
                translate([5, i, 0]) rotate(-45) square(20);
                    translate([0, 23, 0]) square(7);
            }
            translate([7, 20, 0]) square(20);
        }
        translate([-100, -10, 0]) square(100);
    }
}

//The following module actually creates the thread
module rawthread(profile = [[0, 5], [.25, 6], [.5, 6], [.75, 5], [1, 5]],
turns = 5,
    internal = false, fn = 20
) {
    lead = profile[len(profile) - 1][0] - profile[0][0];
    length = turns * lead;
    echo(lead);
    echo(length);
    points = concat(
        [[0, 0, 0]],
        [for(i = [0:len(profile) - 2]) [profile[i][1], 0, profile[i][0]]],
        [for(z = [0:lead:length], a = [360/fn:360/fn:360],
            point = [for(i = [0:len(profile) - 2])
            [profile[i][0], (profile[i][1] + (z + a / 360) *
            (profile[len(profile) - 1][1] - profile[0][1])) *
```

```
            (internal ? 1 / cos(180 / fn) : 1)]])
            [point[1] * cos(a), point[1] * sin(a), z + point[0] + a/360 *
            lead]],
        [[0, 0, length + lead + profile[len(profile) - 2][0] - profile[0][0]]]
    );

    faces = concat(
        [for(i = [0:fn - 1]) [0, i * (len(profile) - 1) + 1, (i + 1) *
    (len(profile) - 1) + 1]],
        [for(i = [0:len(profile) - 2]) [0, (i == len(profile) - 2) ?
        (len(profile) - 1) *
            fn + 1 : i + 2, i + 1]],
        [for(i = [for(z = [0:(turns - 0)], j = [0:len(profile) - 3], a =
        [0:fn - 1])
            quad(
                1 + (z * fn + a) * (len(profile) - 1) + j,
                1 + (z * fn + a) * (len(profile) - 1) + (len(profile) - 1) + j,
                1 + (z * fn + a) * (len(profile) - 1) + ((j == (len(profile)
                - 2)) ?
                fn * (len(profile) - 1) : j + 1) + (len(profile) - 1),
                1 + (z * fn + a) * (len(profile) - 1) + ((j == (len(profile)
                - 2)) ?
                fn * (len(profile) - 1) : j + 1)
            )], v = i) v],//*/
        [for(i = [for(z = [0:turns - 1], j = [len(profile) - 2], a = [0:fn - 1])
            quad(
                1 + (z * fn + a) * (len(profile) - 1) + j,
                1 + (z * fn + a) * (len(profile) - 1) + (len(profile) - 1) + j,
                1 + (z * fn + a) * (len(profile) - 1) + fn * (len(profile) - 1) +
                (len(profile) - 1),
                1 + (z * fn + a) * (len(profile) - 1) + fn * (len(profile) - 1)
            )], v = i) v],//*/
        [for(i = [0:len(profile) - 2]) [len(points) - 1, len(points) - 1,
        len(points) - 1]
            - [0, (i == len(profile) - 2) ? (len(profile) - 1) * fn + 1 :
            i + 2, i + 1]],
                [for(i = [0:fn - 1]) [len(points) - 1, len(points) - 1,
            len(points) - 1] - [0, i * (len(profile) - 1) + 1, (i + 1) *
            (len(profile) - 1) + 1]]
    );
        translate([0, 0, -lead]) polyhedron(points, faces, convexity = 10);
}
function quad(a, b, c, d, r = false) = r ? [[a, b, c], [c, d, a]] :
[[c, b, a], [a, d, c]];
//create triangles from quad
```

Wheel, Axle, and Pulley

A wheel and axle are very similar to a pulley. As a result, we have a model that will generate both, depending on a parameter. We talk about each machine and then introduce the model that creates one or the other (based on setting a variable to `true` or `false`).

Wheel and Axle

The combination of a wheel and axle appears to have been around the longest of all the simple machines. The first known instances were in Mesopotamia between 5,000 and 6,000 years ago. A wheel makes it easier to move things by allowing a large force at the hub to be translated to a smaller motion at the rim, creating mechanical advantage. Wheels also reduce frictional resistance with the ground by having a small contact area with the ground; friction in a wheel occurs at the axle. Wheels also function like a variable-angle inclined plane at their leading and trailing edges as they roll over the ground, smoothing out any bumps in the surface they roll over.

Some ancient civilizations (including the Egyptians) managed engineering feats without the wheel or the pulley. In modernity, wheels are usually seen in combination with other simple machines, like the combination of lever and wheel and axle we see in the humble wheelbarrow (Figure 5-8). The wheel allows the user to move around heavy loads, and the handles (levers) allows hoisting the barrow up onto its wheel. (Otherwise, it rests on its feet.)

Figure 5-8. *Wheel and axle, combined with a lever, in a modern wheelbarrow*

Pulley

A pulley is a wheel and axle with a groove around the wheel's rim. A rope, chain, or belt of some sort goes into the groove and supports a weight. In the simplest form, a pulley just changes the direction of a force, but not its magnitude. The idler pulley in Figure 5-9, for example, changes the direction of the cable running over it, which in turn is pulling around the y-axis of a 3D printer.

Figure 5-9. Idler pulley on a consumer 3D printer

If more than one pulley is used, then the weight of an object is distributed over several sections of rope. A block and tackle and related, more-complex devices exploit this feature. The mechanical advantage depends on the number of pulleys, their distribution, and how the rope is attached—look up "block and tackle" to see some examples (a good one is this Wikipedia article: https://en.wikipedia.org/wiki/Block_and_tackle). The diameter of a pulley typically does not affect its mechanical advantage. The exception is when a pulley's axle is attached to something else, such as a pulley with a different diameter, so that the two turn together.

Wheel and Pulley Models

The same OpenSCAD model creates a sample pair of four wheels on two axles, or an arbitrary string of pulleys on one frame. The variables you can adjust are in Table 5-4, and the model is in Listing 5-4.

Table 5-4. *Wheel and Pulley Variables*

Variable	Default Value and Units	Meaning
wheel	true (wheels) false (pulleys)	Select wheels or pulleys
clearance	0.4 mm	Spacing between wheels or pulleys and hub, must be loose enough to allow free rotation
pulley_width	8 mm	Width for pulleys
wheel_width	20 mm	Width for wheels, should be greater than min_diameter
spacing	3 mm	Between pulleys or wheels
loop	8 mm	Diameter of loop and hook at either end
count	2 mm	Number of pulleys (wheels are always 2)
min_diameter	20 mm	Min size of pulley or wheels
diameter_step	5 mm	How much bigger to make each pulley when doing multiples
csec_d	5 mm	Cross-sectional diameter of pulley frame

■ **Note**   The wheels or pulleys take a while to render in OpenSCAD. Do not close the window while OpenSCAD is calculating and rendering.

Listing 5-4. Wheel and Pulley Model

```
// A model which creates pulleys and wheels on a holder
// Makes one piece for the backbone/hub, then a pulley or wheel
// and a clip to hold each pulley or wheel
// Designed to be printed in several pieces and then assembled
// File pulleysWheels.scad

wheel = false; //wheels = false gives you pulleys
clearance = .4; //spacing between hub and wheel/pulley, mm
pulley_width = 8; // rim, in mm
wheel_width = 20; // rim, in mm - must be greater than min_diameter
spacing = 3; //space between wheel rims or pulley
loop = 8;  //diameter of the loop on one side the the hook on the other, mm
count = 2; // number of pulleys (ignored for wheels)
min_diameter = 20; // minimum acceptable size of pulley or wheels, mm
diameter_step = 5; // how much bigger to make each pulley when doing
                // multiples, mm
csec_d = 5; //cross-sectional diameter of pulley frame, mm
```

```
$fs = .5;  //OpenSCAD facet controls
$fa = 2;   //OpenSCAD facet controls

width = wheel ? wheel_width : pulley_width;
diameter = wheel ? [min_diameter, min_diameter] : [for(x = [0:count - 1])
min_diameter + (count - x - 1) * diameter_step];

if(wheel) {
    %for(i = [0:len(diameter) - 1], j = [0, 1], d = diameter[i]) mirror
([j, 0, 0]) translate([-width/2, center_offset(i), csec_d / 2 * sin(45)])
rotate([0, 90, 0]) wheel(d);
    for(i = [0:len(diameter) - 1], j = [0, 1], d = diameter[i]) translate
([j * -(diameter[i] + 1) - diameter[i]/2 - width/2 - csec_d - spacing - 1,
center_offset(i), 0]) wheel(d);
} else {
    %for(i = [0:len(diameter) - 1], d = diameter[i]) translate([-width/2,
    center_offset(i),
        csec_d / 2 * sin(45)]) rotate([0, 90, 0]) pulley(d);
    for(i = [0:len(diameter) - 1], d = diameter[i]) translate
([-diameter[i]/2 - width/2 - csec_d -
        spacing - 1, center_offset(i), 0]) pulley(d);
}

//create pulley
module pulley(d) difference() {
    rotate_extrude() difference() {
        square([(d + spacing)/2 - clearance, width - clearance * 2 + 1]);
        difference() {
            translate([d/2 + width/2, width/2 - clearance + 1, 0])
                circle(width / sin(45) / 2);
            square([(d + spacing)/2, 1]);
        }
    }
    cylinder(r = (csec_d / 2 + clearance) / cos(180 / 8), h = width *
    3, center = true, $fn = 8);
}

//create wheel
module wheel(d) difference() {
    union() {
        cylinder(r = d/2, h = 3);
        cylinder(r = (csec_d / 2 + clearance + 3) / cos(180 / 8), h = width
/ 2 + .5 - clearance * 1.5, $fn = 8);
    }
    cylinder(r = (csec_d / 2 + clearance) / cos(180 / 8), h = width *
    3, center = true, $fn = 8);
}
```

```
module csec(d = csec_d) translate([0, d/2 * sin(45), 0]) intersection() {
    circle(d/2);
        square([d, d * sin(45)], center = true);
}

module straight(l = 10, center = true, ends = true) {
    rotate([90, 0, 180]) linear_extrude(height = l, center = center,
convexity = 5) csec();
    if(ends) for(b = center ? [1/2, -1/2] : [0, 1]) translate([0, b, 0])
arc(0);
}

module arc(r = 10, a = 360, ends = true) union() {
    intersection() {
        linear_extrude(height = csec_d, convexity = 5) {
            if(a < 90) intersection_for(b = [0, a - 90]) rotate(b)
            square(r + csec_d);
            else for(b = [0:45:a]) rotate(min(b, a - 90)) square
            (r + csec_d);
        }
        rotate_extrude(convexity = 5) intersection() {
            translate([r, 0, 0]) csec();
            square(r + csec_d);
        }
    }
    if(a < 360 && ends) for(b = [0, a]) rotate(b) translate([r, 0, 0]) arc(0);
}

function center_offset(n) = (n == 0) ? 0 : [for(i = [0:n - 1]) diameter[i]/2
+ spacing + diameter[i+1]/2 * [for(i = [0:n - 1]) 1];

//create snap rings to retain wheels/pulleys
for(i = [0:len(diameter) - 1]) translate([(width + csec_d) / 2 - csec_d * 1.5,
    center_offset(i) - csec_d * 1.5 - 1, 0]) linear_extrude(2) difference()
{
    circle(csec_d);
    rotate(180 / 8) circle((csec_d / 2 * sin(45) + clearance / 2) / cos(180
    / 8), $fn = 8);
    translate([0, -csec_d/2 - csec_d * sin(45) / 2 - 2, 0]) square([csec_d *
    2, csec_d], center = true);
    translate([0, csec_d, 0]) square([csec_d * sin(45) * .9, csec_d * 2],
    center = true);
    translate([0, csec_d * 1.2, 0]) scale([1, 2, 1]) rotate(45)
square(csec_d, center = true);
}
```

```
//create backbone and axles
translate([(width + csec_d) / 2 + 1, -diameter[0]/2, 0])
    straight(diameter[0]/2 + center_offset(len(diameter) - 1) +
diameter[len(diameter) - 1]/2, false);
for(i = [0:len(diameter) - 1]) translate([(width + csec_d) / 2 + 1, center_
offset(i), 0]) rotate(90) {
    difference() {
        straight(width + csec_d + clearance + 2, center = false);
        translate([0, ((width + csec_d) / 2 + 1 + clearance) + width/2,
csec_d / 2 * sin(45)]) rotate([-90, 0, 0]) linear_extrude(2 + clearance * 2)
difference() {
            circle(csec_d);
            circle(csec_d / 2 * sin(45));
        }
    }
    rotate([90, 0, 180]) linear_extrude(height = csec_d / 2 + clearance,
    center = false,
        convexity = 5) translate([0, csec_d/2 * sin(45), 0]) intersection() {
        circle(csec_d/2 + 1);
        square([csec_d + 2, csec_d * sin(45)], center = true);
    }
}

// create the end loop and hook
for(i = [0, 1]) mirror([0, i, 0]) translate([0, i ? diameter[0] / 2 :
center_offset(len(diameter) - 1) +
    diameter[len(diameter) - 1]/2, 0]) {
    arc((width + csec_d)/2 + 1, 90);

    translate([0, width / 2 + csec_d + 1 + loop/2, 0]) rotate(30)
        arc(csec_d/2 + loop/2, i ? 240 : 360);
}
```

Assembling and Using Wheel and Pulley Models

These models need a bit of assembly. Figure 5-10 is a set of wheels on the printer bed. Figure 5-11 is a one-pulley set and a two-pulley set printed at the same time. Figure 5-12 is the assembled wheel set, and Figure 5-13, the pulleys. The wheels (or pulleys) go on their axles and then are secured with the small C-shaped clips.

Figure 5-10. *Wheel pieces, as printed*

Figure 5-11. *One-pulley and two-pulley set, as printed together (two OpenSCAD runs)*

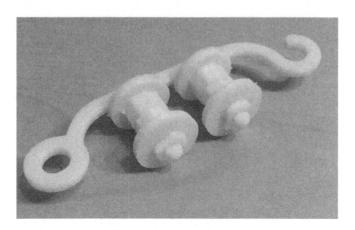

Figure 5-12. *The wheels printed in Figure 5-10, assembled*

Figure 5-13. *The pulleys printed in Figure 5-11, assembled*

Obviously, if you want to demonstrate wheels, there are any number of pull-toys you can use. Our entry here is intended to be a base that you can add to or scale for specific demonstrations. You can play with various surfaces and explore how much friction is needed for something to roll (versus sliding), for example.

We talked about pulley mechanical advantage earlier in this section. Figure 5-14 shows a block and tackle (one of many designs) assembled from the pulleys in Figure 5-13 (and only using one of the pulleys on the double set).

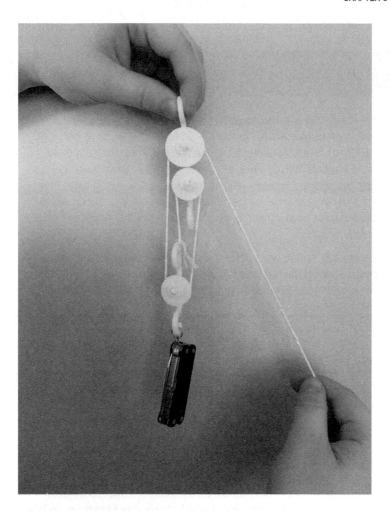

Figure 5-14. *Block and tackle*

Printing Suggestions

These models can be scaled up (made bigger), but only the wedge and inclined plane can safely be made smaller. The other models may have tolerance issues if they are made too small. The screw model is something of a precision part, and we suggest that you print it only in the orientation that the current OpenSCAD model creates. Generally it will be better to change the scaling variables in OpenSCAD than to use 3D printer software scaling functions.

We have a picture of each of the models as-printed and an additional one of the model in use for the more dynamic models. Depending on your print bed size you may be able to print several at once. Each model also had a list of the parameters you can save easily.

We printed all these models in PLA, without support, typically with about 15% infill.

THINKING ABOUT THESE MODELS: LEARNING LIKE A MAKER

Unlike many of the other models in this book, these did not start with an abstraction. Rather, they are prints of things that are normally 3-dimensional objects. In the course of creating them, we did not struggle to think about how to represent them, since the objects are physical already. Here, the challenge is that these building blocks are normally part of more complex wholes. You will need to spend some time thinking about what you want to learn (or teach) from these models to decide which ones to print out and how to arrange them to do something useful or to demonstrate a principle.

Mechanical advantage can, for the most part, be shown with a string taped to a weight (a few coins, possibly). The previous talks about the issues of matching scale and integrating these into more-complex models. We encourage you to try these out and see what you can construct.

Where to Learn More

Since simple machines are a required topic in many elementary and middle school curricula, there are correspodingly large numbers of online games and student and teacher support materials available online. Try searching for *simple machine games.* We were particularly charmed by ones from the Museum of Science and Industry in Chicago (www.msichicago.org/play/simplemachines/) and another from the group Edheads (www.edheads.org/activities/simple-machines/). These videos use common items to demonstrate or identify simple machines.

The definition of *simple machines* is a little arbitrary. Different disciplines have varying opinions about what the simple machines include. Sometimes gears are included as a distinct seventh simple machine; others feel that meshing gears are really a wheel and axle combined with wedges. Either way, there are already a lot of fun gears available to 3D print, so we will not add to the supply. Search *gears* on www.thingiverse.com, but be careful to check the comments to see if the design has actually been proven out.

If you are feeling like trying something a little harder, you can try Rich's quick print gear bearing (Figure 5-15) instructions at www.youmagine.com/designs/quick-print-gear-bearing (based on one by Emmett Lalish, at www.thingiverse.com/thing:53451). These gears (a set of planetary gears) print very fast relative to other 3D-printable gears and are fun for demonstrations. They are a little tricky though—you are printing the *hollow spaces in*side the model, not the model surface itself (Figure 5-16). This can be done with creative use of slicing program settings. The gears come off the printer ready to turn once you wiggle them a little to free them up.

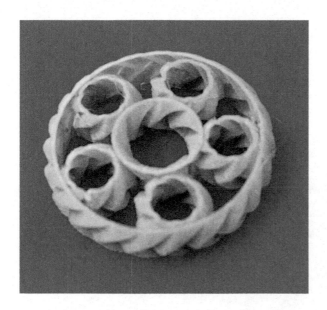

Figure 5-15. *Rich's quick print gear (prints assembled, just as shown)*

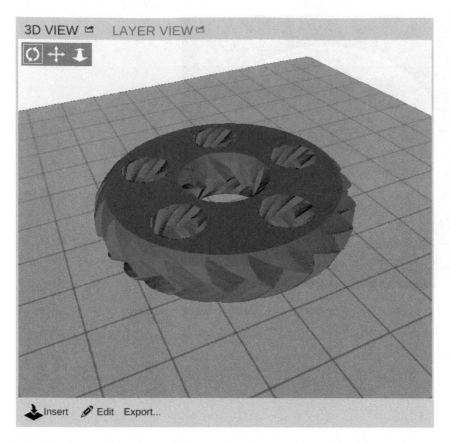

Figure 5-16. *What the model looks like in MatterControl—you are printing the empty space, not the modeled surface*

Our book *3D Printing with MatterControl* uses printing this gear as an advanced slicing exercise (Figures 5-15 through 5-17 are from Chapter 10 of that book). Figure 5-17 gives the MatterControl preset that works with these gears, assuming you are using MatterSlice. Appendix A talks more about MatterControl in general.

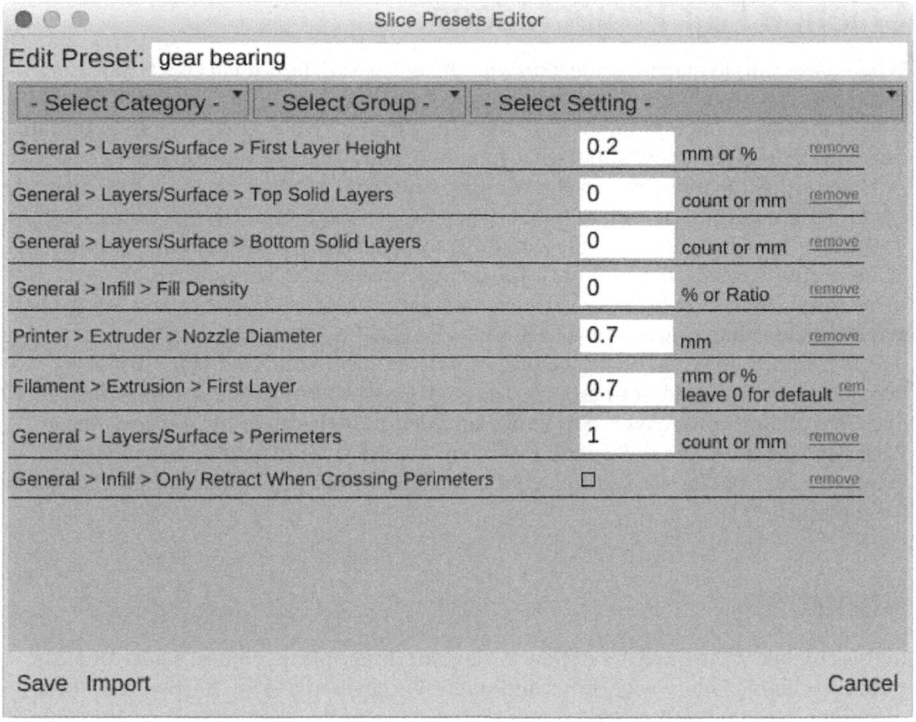

Figure 5-17. *Rich's quick print gear settings in MatterControl*

Teacher Tips

Since simple machines are so ubiquitous, one simple thing to do is to have students look around at common household or classroom objects and deconstruct them to find the simple machines. Kitchen hand tools are particularly rich sources of machines. These everyday hand tools can be surprisingly complex. Then you can have students design their own combinations of simple machines to solve some theme or problem.

Some schools have given students projects to recreate historic machines, sometimes with a twist. For example, Castilleja School's Bourne Idea Lab (www.castilleja.org/bournidealab) had students recreate some of Leonardo DaVinci's machines, with some modern twists.

Generally the topics around simple machines are covered in the NGSS Forces and Interactions standards (MS-PS-2, www.nextgenscience.org/msps2-motion-stability-forces-interactions) and Energy standards (MS-PS-3, www.nextgenscience.org/msps3-energy). University of Colorado, Boulder also has a set of lesson plans, with alignment to various standards, at www.teachengineering.org/view_lesson.php?url=collection/cub_/lessons/cub_simp_machines/cub_simp_machines_lesson01.xml.

Science Fair Project Ideas

When these simple machines meet up with the real world, non-ideal effects like friction come into play. You might characterize some of these real-world effects and find a systematic way to manage them to minimize inefficiency. Analyze what existing products do to be efficient and think about what you might change to do something better.

Getting a little more into product design issues, you might think about how machines meant for humans to use without additional power (hand tools, daily-use objects) might be more or less efficient for people with different size hands or in different environments (for example, wearing gloves or not). You could also look into what kinds of things make these simple machines break or not work very well, and what enhancements are the best shields against that.

Some good books on both good user experience design and the origins of classic mechanisms are Donald Norman's *The Design of Everyday Things* (Basic Paperbacks, 2002) and Henry Petroski's books on how things fail when good design principles are violated. Petroski's classic work is *To Engineer Is Human: The Role of Failure in Successful Design* (Vintage, 1992), but he also has entire books focused on a few particular inventions, such as the toothpick.

Summary

In this chapter, we learned about how to 3D print six simple machines: wheel and axle, pulley, inclined plane, wedge, lever, and screw. We covered a bit of the history of these machines, how they generate mechanical advantage, and how to print them. We wound up with some ideas on how to demonstrate the idea of a simple machine with historical recreations, or perhaps some research into good product design.

CHAPTER 6

■ ■ ■

Plants and Their Ecosystems

When we think about plants, *dynamic* is not usually a word that comes to mind. Plants are part of the landscape. Unless you are a gardener, you might never give the trees and smaller plants around you a second thought. The fact that plants are, well, planted in place has some evolutionary implications, though. If you are a life form that cannot move (other than by growing vertically or spreading horizontally), and the environment around you changes, your offspring have the options of adapting or dying out. This means that plants have developed a wild array of forms to follow their ecological niche function.

This chapter develops a model of how plants grow to take in as much sunlight as possible and to manage water and other resources, and how this function might need to vary in different ecosystems. Our intent is that you will play with the model and create yourself some plant communities to print out and think about. This chapter can therefore be approached at many different levels: from creating flower and plant models for elementary students, to thinking about "evolving" a plant for an ecosystem, or to looking at the mathematics underlying the model.

Botany Background

Botany, the study of plants, is one of the oldest sciences. Everyone who either forages for or farms plants will do better the more they have predictive power about what plant will grow where, and how to encourage plants that have the best potential as a food source.

If an animal's habitat changes, it can adapt (on evolutionary time scales of millennia) or migrate somewhere else. Plants, however, cannot move in the same way. They can hitchhike to another climate by spreading seeds, but often a species that does not adapt fast enough will just die out.

Wikipedia says there are somewhere between 300,000 and 315,000 species of plants (https://en.wikipedia.org/wiki/Plant). However, as a result of ecosystem destruction coupled with climate changing rapidly, the rate of extinction is very high. Just how high is a matter of some intense debate, but most reports assume double-digit percentages of plants may be gone in the next century.

Add to that many invasive species, which are spread to new habitats accidentally or deliberately as people jet around the planet. These factors mean that it is important to think about plants as part of an overall ecosystem, and consider how the plants and resources in an area play together.

To thrive, plants need the right amount of six things: light, water, gasses, temperature, mineral nutrients, and mechanical support. We are going to focus on just two of those—light and water—and talk about how plants fit into environments where one of those is limited.

Water

Plants need water both for their chemical reactions and the majority of their structures. However, plants that receive too much water can rot. Therefore, plants in wet environments like jungles and rainforests have developed strategies to get rid of water, like waxy leaves that come to a point to drip away water.

On the other hand, desert plants work pretty hard to both hang on to water and to keep animals and insects from chomping on the structures they managed to create with their hard-won water. Desert plants often have a milky, acid sap (notably plants in the genus *Euphorbia,* commonly called *spurge*). This sap will squirt out on anything that chances taking a bite out of a *euphorb* to get some moisture. Other desert plants have spines or spikes to discourage nibbling, like the agave in Figure 6-1, as well as tough outer surfaces that hold water in and keep it from evaporating in desert summer sun.

Figure 6-1. *Agave spines and tough outer surface defend their hard-earned moisture*

Sunlight

Plants, for the most part, make their living by capturing the sun's energy in chemical bonds. Too little sun, and a plant may fail to thrive and reproduce. However, some plants cannot handle too much sun and have evolved to live in the shadow of other plants. Plants can get sunburned, too.

Nutrients

Nitrogen is a very abundant element. Plants need nitrogen to grow and typically get it from the soil. Plants are also dependent to one degree or another on many other elements, such as potassium and phosphorus, for different functions. Some plants put needed elements back in the soil so that other plants can use them (like "nitrogen-fixing" plants such as fava beans). Others die if soil has too high a concentration of elements that might be needed for another plant.

If you are a gardener and buy fertilizer, you will often see it labeled with numbers like 8-0-24. The first number (in this case, 8) is the percentage of nitrogen by weight in the preparation. The second (zero, here) is the percentage of available phosphate (P_2O_5), and the third (24 in our example) represents soluble potash (potassium in water-soluble form, K_2O). These are usually called NPK values, since K is the chemical symbol for the element potassium. Different fertilizers are sold because different plants may need different combinations of nutrients from each other. Even the same plant may need different fertilizer at different points in its lifecycle, and may need trace nutrients too.

Plant Communities

When you create a garden, you need to consider whether the chemistry, water, and sun needs of plants you put next to each other are compatible. In natural environments, evolution takes care of which plants survive and which do not, which brings us to the topic of how plants form communities. Figure 6-2 shows a typical cooperative ecosystem of *Camellia japonica* and cocculus.

Camellia japonica bushes evolved in a cool climate in Asia and were transplanted to the southwestern United States, where they flower in winter in the shade of other trees. The trees above get all the sun they want, and the camellias flourish in their shade and leaf litter. (If camellias are out in the sun in Southern California in the summer, the leaves get blotchy sunburn where they are exposed.)

Figure 6-2. *Camellia japonica bushes shaded by cocculus trees in February, Pasadena, California*

    Camellias originated in Asia; the tree is native to the Himalayas. This camellia's cousin, *Camellia sinensis*, is known best as the plant that gives us tea. Yet together (as in Figure 6-2) they thrive in Southern California, in a Mediterranian climate.

    This is an example of how plants compete with each other for resources like sun, but also may cooperate. A plant (like these camellias) that cannot handle much sun or wind might have the best chance for survival under a tree. Some plants might need different nutrients than others, and so can grow close together without depleting the soil—one plant might even deposit nutrients another needs. Some plants deposit chemicals in the soil that prevent other plants from germinating. Others try to outdo each other with attractive flowers to attract more pollinating insects and birds.

All plants grow and reproduce, either in competition or cooperation with one another, in the soil in which they sprouted. As the environment around them changes, they adapt or die out. In this chapter, we show some of the mathematics of plant growth and develop some simple models of plant leaves and flowers. Then you can think about how you might use these models to think about an entire ecosystem and how it is affected when things change.

The Mathematics of Plant Growth

When a plant adds growth on to itself, usually the new material is layered on at a part of the plant called the *meristem*. It would be a waste of the plant's energy and biomass if the leaves were mostly covered by other leaves, or if all the petals of a flower (meant to attract pollinators) were in a big pile rather than spread out as broadly as possible to let bees and hummingbirds know that the buffet is on the table.

Evolution has favored plants that have the most efficient distribution of leaves and flower petals. As it turns out, this efficient distribution spaces subsequent leaves or petals by the *golden angle* (about 137.52 degrees). The story of this angle is closely related to numbers called the *Fibonacci sequence*. We talk about all that in the next sections, and then use this model in the rest of the chapter as the basis for our 3D-printed plant models.

The Golden Ratio

Two numbers, *a* and *b*, with *b* the larger number, are said to be in *the golden ratio* to each other if $(a + b)/b = b/a$. If that's true, then the ratio of a/b is equal to the golden ratio.

■ **Note** The golden ratio is exactly equal to (1+ sqrt(5))/2, or about 1.618. It is usually referred to by the Greek letter φ (phi), most commonly pronounced "fie" in the English-speaking world, but "fee" in Greek and by some mathematicians and physicists. It has some other interesting properties, like this recursive definition:

$$\phi = 1 + (1/\phi)$$

φ is an irrational number (like pi), which means that you can never write down all its digits, because there is no pattern as there is for, say, 2/3. The ancient Greeks and Egyptians knew about it and used it in art (to scale the sides of the pyramids, for example), since the proportion 1:1.618 feels pleasing to the eye. There is a good extensive explanation with pictures at www.mathsisfun.com/numbers/golden-ratio.html.

The Golden Angle

Suppose you went around a circle 1.618 (or φ) times. There are 360 degrees in a circle, so that would be 584.2 degrees. If you go 360 degrees, or 720 degrees, you wind up back where you started. Suppose we subtract 584.2 degrees from 720 degrees to see how short we are from going around twice. That winds up being roughly 137.52 degrees, which is called the golden angle.

■ **Note**   If you want to lay out something around a circle such that every time you go around you put something down a little different place than the last time, one way to ensure that is to space things out by multiples of the golden angle. Because it is not possible to write down the golden angle exactly (since it is an irrational number), each subsequent placement will be just a bit off in relation to its predecessors. Plants have evolved in many cases to lay out their material in ways that are very similar to this, as we will see shortly.

Fibonacci Sequence

Closely related to the concept of the golden ratio is the Fibonacci sequence, credited to the Italian mathematician Fibonacci, who published them in 1212 to try and model the breeding of rabbits. He failed in that, since populations follow a different relationship, but nevertheless laid the groundwork for a lot of other mathematics.

   The Fibonacci sequence is defined such that it begins either with {0, 1} or {1, 1} (depending on whom you ask), and that if you add any two consecutive numbers in the sequence, you get the next number. The sequence is: {(0,) 1, 1, 2, 3, 5, 8, 13, 21, 34, 55 . . .}. If you divide a number in the sequence by the prior one, you get: {1/1, 2/1, 3/2, 8/5, 13/8, 21/13, 34/21, 55/34 . . .} or {1, 2, 1.5, 1.600, 1.625, 1.615, 1.619, 1.618 . . .}, which as you can see is getting closer and closer to the golden ratio, 1.618 (rounded to four digits). Mathematicians have shown that the ratio of consecutive numbers in this sequence approaches the golden ratio as the numbers get bigger and bigger. You can read the article at https://en.wikipedia.org/wiki/Fibonacci_number if you want to learn more.

Phyllotaxis

The process of *phyllotaxis* generates leaves in a growing plant. Leaves are where the plant makes a living—taking sunlight and water and creating the sugars the plant needs to live and reproduce. Leaves are generated at the plant's meristem, usually at the tip of a stem or branch, which has specialized cells that produce new plant material.

As mentioned earlier, if plants just popped one leaf out under another, then the leaves above would block sunlight from the ones below. If the leaves were regularly spaced (say at 90-degree angles) then at least some of the leaves would overlap. What you really want (if you are a plant) is to have a sequence that never quite repeats and places leaves evenly around your center.

As it turns out, placing subsequent leaves at the golden angle accomplishes this, since no two leaves will quite line up. Many plants have a number of leaves or flower petals corresponding to the Fibonacci sequence of numbers (many with 5 or 8 leaves or petals).

If the leaves are pushing out of a center and forming new leaves that push out old ones (or form on the outside of the old ones), a spiral pattern arises. There are various different spiral patterns in nature, including Archimedean spirals and logarithmic ones. In our model here, we are implementing a very simplistic spiral with a linearly increasing radius to give an easy-to-describe starting point for your explorations. You might consider modifying the model we will introduce here to try out different ways of thinking about plant growth.

The Models

The models in this chapter attempt to generate somewhat stylized plants and flowers following the mathematics in the preceding section. We have developed two different OpenSCAD models. One can generate desert plants and flowers, and the other can handle jungle plants. The models have many parameters to govern how the leaves or petals are angled and spaced but maintain the overall spiral arrangement (and use a Fibonacci-number number of petals or leaves). As we talk about in the "Learning Like a Maker" section later on, it is interesting what complex behavior a relatively simple rule can generate and why we needed to separate these two models.

To generate each leaf/petal, Rich recycled some of the concepts used to create the airfoil cross-sections in Chapter 4. You will see some strong similarities in the code in this chapter and the basic airfoil simulation there. Next, we tried to start with first principles, and think about what kind of plant would likely do well in a particular environment—and then see how close our plants were to real ones in the ecosystem.

We think that these models may be a fun way to focus discussion on how plant form evolves based on its ecosystem and needs. You might think about designing a community, and then trying to find and model most disruptive invasive species that could possibly up-end this community. This design is not really suitable for creating trees, but you might think about how some of the principles might apply.

For floral simulations, you might think about what type of pollinator is present in the environment and create an arrangement that is as friendly as possible. Then see if your design matches actual plants in the ecosystem, and see whether nature evolved something even more interesting than you came up with. Then you can try "evolving" your own model to see what sort of solutions to plant problems you come up with.

■ **Note**   The models in this chapter are not intended to be precise models of any given plant. Rather, they are a demonstration of how relatively simple rules can create models that can show some broad principles of plant growth. The realities of plant evolution are complex; we suggest further reading at the end of the chapter. That said, we think that creating a plant from first principles to live in an environment is an exercise that gives some unusual insight into the problems plants (and home gardeners) deal with every day. This section shows you examples of what the code can do. Then, in the next section, we talk about how we created these, and how you can create models of your own.

Desert Plants

The first plant we tried to print out was a desert plant, like an aloe or agave. Figure 6-3 shows our print next to the real thing. Desert plants tend to have their leaves or other major parts arranged so that water will run right down to their roots if it rains, and thus are relatively easy to print, with limited overhangs.

Figure 6-3. *3D-printed aloe model next to its real cousin*

However, this model was challenging to print because the leaves became very thin at the top, and printers have difficulty printing sparse, thin material at the top of a print, so we tended to get a bit of stringing. Figure 6-4 shows the model completed. The drooled bits can be trimmed off carefully with small pointed scissors or another tool. Wear eye protection because the bits tend to fly around when you snip them off.

Figure 6-4. *The finished aloe (with a bit of stringing)*

Tropical Jungle Plants

Plants that live in a hot, wet environment have to deal with an opposite set of problems from their cousins who live in a desert. In a hot, wet environment, plants are so dense that the biggest competition is for light. Brian Capon's book *Plant Survival* (Timber Press, 1994) says that only about 5% of the light falling on the forest canopy makes it to the forest floor, which means that often there are not a lot of plants on the forest floor.

■ **Note**   Many houseplants (such as philodendrons) evolved in a tropical jungle environment, where they survived with little light and the ability to handle being overwatered. Figure 6-5 is a large philodendron, commonly known as the lacy tree.

The other problem a jungle plant faces is avoiding having so much water around that the plant rots. Some plants make a living hanging off trees (such as *ephiphytes*) and get their moisture from the air. Plants develop waxy leaves and "drip tips" on the leaves to shed water, like the calla lily leaf in Figure 6-6. (Note that waxy leaves can keep water in, too, and are not limited to jungle plants.) Since many jungle plants are spindly (to get maximum light) and have big curved leaves, they are challenging to model with a 3D print. The leaves want to be nearly parallel to the sun to capture as much light coming down as possible, though, so we can print the leaves nearly flat, as we will see in a minute.

Figure 6-5. *Lacy tree (Philodendron bipinnatifidum) enjoying a damp, shady corner of a Southern California yard*

Because of the water-shedding downward tips of a typical jungle leaf, these plants required a different model than the desert ones. This model creates the leaves one at a time and creates a base with stems that allows you to lay out the stems in a spiral pattern and print big, flat leaves separately. We talk about the models in detail (and provide listings and settings) in the "Using These Models" section later in the chapter.

Figure 6-6. *Leaves of a plant native to a a wet environment*

Figure 6-7 shows how the jungle plant model appears on a printer bed (printed with one extra leaf for display purposes), and Figure 6-8 shows it assembled. If you were creating an ecosystem, you would most likely glue the leaves in place (and probably glue the base to the bottom of any display you were creating). If you wanted the leaves to be a little more horizontal, you could accomplish that with a bit of glue.

Figure 6-7. *Plant with drip-tip leaves, on the printer*

117

Figure 6-8. *Assembled version of the model in Figure 6-7, showing the leaves' finer structures*

Figure 6-9 is a photo of the jungle plant model taken from above (similar to the photo of the real plant in Figure 6-5 or 6-6.) Notice how well the leaves fill the space (and how little one leaf shades another.

Figure 6-9. *The jungle plant model from above on a sunny day*

Flowers

Plants make their food through photosynthesis, using water and solar energy converted by their leaves. But they also need to keep their species going. Some plants reproduce by sending out runners or budding-off pieces, cloning themselves. Others need to have pollen moved around from male flower parts to female ones. To do that, certain types of plants (*angiosperms*) have evolved flowers to attract and guide pollinators.

As with leaves, it is an advantage to a plant to use the energy to make a flower as efficiently as possible. In the case of a flower, the job is to get the attention of a pollinator (like a bee) and attract it into the flower so that the pollinator gets coated with pollen, which then gets carried to another flower for pollination.

As you can see in Figures 6-10 and 6-11, both the formal *Camellia japonica* blossom and the lowly (some might say weedy) lawn daisy have their petals splayed out for maximum display. We used the same mathematics to create the flowers as we did for the aloes, with some different values for variables, which we talk about in the "Using These Models" section.

Figure 6-10. *Two species of C. japonica. The upper one is not yet fully open*

Figure 6-11. *Lawn daisies*

Figure 6-12 shows the camellia model (printed without support), and Figure 6-13 and 6-14, the daisy. You can see that this simple model replicates a lot of the structure, although obviously no model this simple will be a perfect one. In the next section, we tie together these models and talk about how to create new plants and flowers with them. Note that these models required some *support*—a 3D printer builds up these models from the bottom, and petals that are nearly horizontal need to have some support material printed below them so that the petals or leaves are not printed in air.

Figure 6-12. *3D-printed camellia model*

Figure 6-13. *3D-printed daisy model on the platform, showing support*

Figure 6-14. *3D-printed daisy in the field*

Printing the Models

Two models collectively generated everything in the last section. The first one, in Listing 6-1, created the plants with leaves attached at the plant base (like the aloe) and the flowers. Listing 6-1, with appropriate parameters, also created the base and stems for jungle plants. The leaves, petals, or stems, as the case may be, are laid out in the spiral we described in the earlier section "The Mathematics of Plant Growth." Listing 6-2 generates one jungle plant leaf—the model had to be different, since these leaves are relatively flat and horizontal, which would require a lot of support material to print on their stems.

The models assume that the leaves or petals spiral out from a center. How tightly they spiral, whether any space is left in the center, whether they tilt or get bigger as they spiral out, and similar considerations are controlled by several variables that you can tweak to create models of different plants.

Plant and Flower Models

The plant/flower model creates a petal/leaf that draws on the curved, variable-thickness model we created for airfoils in Chapter 4. Then this leaf is duplicated and each new leaf is rotated, stretched, and offset to build up the model. In the case of the jungle plant stems, the parameters listed in Table 6-1 will give you stems, on which you can hang the leaves created in Listing 6-1. The OpenSCAD model variables you can change in Listing 6-1 are as follows:

- length: The length of each petal (mm). However, the model will stretch the petals horizontally (along the radius) while shortening them vertically, based on the value of some of the other variables.

- width: The base width of each petal (mm). Depending on other variables, this should be roughly the width of the leaf at its widest point.

- thickness: The thickness of each petal as a percentage of width.

- pointiness: A parameter that should be greater than zero but not exceed 1, defining the shape of the end of the leaf. A value of 1 will make a leaf with a pointed tip, while a value close to 0 will make a leaf that is almost circular.

- curvature: A parameter that controls how much the petals curve outward as their number increases. The range for this number will depend on how many petals you have as well as the size of the gap in the center (if any), but you're unlikely to need a value larger than about 5. If your outer petals get really long and flat as they radiate horizontally, decrease this number.

- shorten: How much to squash down (in the vertical direction) the outer leaves relative to the inner ones. If things start pointing downward around the outside of the plant, shorten is too big.

- petals: Number of petals. Should be a number in the Fibonacci sequence (see discussion earlier in the chapter).

- petalSpacing: Radial offset of each petal relative to the next one (cumulative, mm).

- openness: Incremental angle (cumulative, in degrees) of how much each subsequent petal is bent down at its base relative to the previous petal.

- petalOffset: Skip this many petals in the center, which creates an open space and a flatter flower.

- tip: Diameter of the leaf tip, in mm. Should usually be 0 unless you want the end of the petal to have some minimum width (such as for adding the drip leaves).

■ **Caution** Table 6-1 gives the values of model variables for the test cases earlier in the chapter. These variables strongly interact with each other to change the geometry. Be sure you look carefully at the model visualization in OpenSCAD and in MatterControl (or your 3D printer's equivalent program) before committing to a print. Some combinations may create conditions that will at best be difficult to print, and at worst may crash OpenSCAD. Do not give up too easily in OpenSCAD, though, because the rendering can take a while—half an hour or so—even on a new laptop. Always use OpenSCAD's preview function to quickly visualize what your model will look like before attempting the slower render function.

■ **Caution** Since many of the variables have open-ended values, it was not possible to exhaustively test the system. We suggest you start with one of the examples in Table 6-1 and then tweak the variables to get the plant you would like. If you get very big outer petals/leaves, decrease the curvature value. These models aim to mimic the general appearance of plants, not capture their process of adding leaves or detailed structure of petal and leaf attachment.

Table 6-1. *Values of the Variables for the Examples in This Chapter*

Variable	Aloe	Daisy	Camellia	Jungle Stem
length	50	50	30	120
width	6	3	3	3
thickness	0.3	0.3	0.1	1
pointiness	0.5	0.2	0.1	1
curvature	1	0.25	0.2	3
shorten	3	0.25	15	6.5
petals	34	21	89	8
petalSpacing	0.4	0.4	0.2	0.2
openness	0.2	0.9	0.1	0.2
petalOffset	10	30	21	13
tip	0	0	0	3

■ **Note**   The daisy model as shown in Figures 6-13 and 6-14 was printed at 90% of the size the variables shown in Table 6-1 would generate. The others were printed at the size naturally generated by these values.

Listing 6-1. Flowers and Plants with Leaves Growing from the Base

```
// OpenSCAD model to create plants and flowers in a modified Archimedes spiral
// File name: FlowersPlants.scad

length = 30; //base petal length (will be modified), mm
width = 3; //base width, mm
thickness = .1; //base thickness, percentage
pointiness = .1; //should be between 0 and 1 - pointier leaves have higher value
curvature = 0.2; //makes the petals bend more
shorten = 15; //makes the petals get shorter from the center out
petals = 89; //needs to be a Fibonacci number (1,2,3,5,8,13,21,34,55,89...)
petalSpacing = .2; //radial offset of each petal (cumulative)
openness = .1; //angle of each petal (cumulative)
petalOffset = 21; //skip this many petals in the center, creates an open
                  // space and flatter flower
tip = 0; //diameter of tip
minbase = 20; //minimum base diameter in mm -increase if your base is too small
```

```
zseg = 20; //vertical segments, more = smoother, but longer rendering
xseg = 10; //horizontal segments, more = smoother, but longer rendering

goldenAngle = 137.508; //constant, should never change

function chord(z) = max(tip / width / 2, sqrt(z) * sqrt(1 - z) * 4 *
pow(1 - z * pointiness, 2) *
    pow(1 / pointiness, 1/3));
function camber(x, a = .5, b = 1) = a * (cos(x * 180 * b) + 1) / 2;
function theta(x, a = .5, b = 1) = a * -sin(x * 180 * b) * 60;
function thickness(x, a = 1, b = thickness) = a * pow(x + 1, 2) *
pow(x - 1, 2) / 10 +
    b * (sqrt(1 + x) + sqrt(1 - x) - 1);

$fs = .5;
$fa = 2;

function quad(a, b, c, d, r = false) = r ? [[a, b, c], [c, d, a]] :
[[c, b, a], [a, d, c]]; //create triangles from quad

function points(roll = 2) = concat([for(i = [for(z = [for(z = [0:zseg])
z / zseg])
  concat(
    [for(
      x = [for(i = [-xseg:xseg]) i / xseg],
      a = chord(z) * (x + thickness(x) * sin(theta(x, .1, chord(z) / 2))),
      r = max(.1,
        (chord(z) * (camber(x, .1, chord(z) / 2) - thickness(x)) *
          cos(theta(x, .1, chord(z) / 2))) + roll + curvature *
          pow(z * roll, 2)
      )
    ) [
      (sin(min(max(a * 180 / PI / r, -179), 179))) * r,
      (cos(min(max(a * 180 / PI / r, -179), 179))) * r - roll,
      z
    ]],
    [for(
      x = [for(i = [-xseg:xseg]) i / xseg],
      a = chord(z) * (-x + thickness(x) * sin(theta(x, .1, chord(z) / 2))),
      r = max(.1,
        (chord(z) * (camber(x, .1, chord(z) / 2) + thickness(x)) *
          cos(theta(x, .1, chord(z) / 2))) + roll + curvature *
          pow(z * roll, 2)
      )
    ) [
      (sin(min(max(a * 180 / PI / r, -179), 179))) * r,
      (cos(min(max(a * 180 / PI / r, -179), 179))) * r - roll,
      z
```

```
    ]]
  )
], j = i) j]);

faces = concat(
  [for(i = [for(x = [0:xseg * 2], xmax = xseg * 4 + 1)
    quad(
      x,
      x + 1,
      xmax - x - 1,
      xmax - x,
      true
    )], v = i) v],
  [for(i = [for(z = [0:zseg - 1], x = [0:xseg * 4 + 1], xmax = xseg * 4 + 2)
    quad(
      z * xmax + x,
      z * xmax + x + xmax,
      z * xmax + x + (((x % xmax) == xmax - 1) ? 0 : xmax) + 1,
      z * xmax + x + (((x % xmax) == xmax - 1) ? -xmax : 0) + 1,
      true
    )], v = i) v],
  [for(i = [for(x = [0:xscg * 2], xmax = xseg * 4 + 1)
    quad(
      len(points()) - 1 - (x),
      len(points()) - 1 - (x + 1),
      len(points()) - 1 - (xmax - x - 1),
      len(points()) - 1 - (xmax - x),
      true
    )], v = i) v]
);
// Create the petals and then distribute them around a modified spiral of
// Archimedes
for(petal = [petalOffset:petalOffset + petals - 1]) rotate([0, 0, petal *
goldenAngle])
  translate([0, petal * petalSpacing, 0]) rotate([-petal * openness, 0, 0])
scale([
    width,
    width,
    length * (1 - pow(petal * openness * curvature * shorten / 100, 3))
  ]) polyhedron(points(petal * petalSpacing / width), faces);

//Create the base
translate([0, 0, -width / 2])
  scale(max(minbase, ((petalOffset + petals) * petalSpacing + width)) / 50)
intersection() {
    scale([1, 1, .5]) sphere(50);
    translate([0, 0, 50]) cube(100, center = true);
  }
```

Jungle Plant Leaf Model

Listing 6-2 generates jungle plant leaves which have a connector that hooks onto the base and stems generated by the model in Listing 6-1 (with appropriate parameters). The variables in Listing 6-2 are as follows:

- size: Length of the leaf from drip tip to base (mm)

- hole: Size of the opening in the connector (mm)

- waviness: How wavy the outer boundary of the leaf is, from 0 (not wavy) to 1 (example shown in Figure 6-8)

■ **Note**   The jungle leaves and stems in Figures 6-7 through 6-9 were printed from the models in Listing 6-1 (with the jungle parameters from Table 6-1) and multiple copies of the leaf generated by Listing 6-2.

Listing 6-2. Jungle Plant Leaves

```
// OpenSCAD model to create one leaft with a "drip tip"
// File name: dripleaf.scad

size = 50;
hole = 4;
waviness = 1;

linear_extrude(.6) scale(size / 25) for(j = [0, 1]) mirror([j, 0, 0]) for(_i =
[for(i = [0:100]) i / 100])
  hull() for(i = [_i, _i + 1/100]) translate([0, pow(i, 2) * 10, 0])
rotate(180 * sqrt(i))
    scale([.1, pow(i, .5) * 10 - (-cos(i * 10 * 360) + 1) * waviness])
rotate(-135) square();
#linear_extrude(1) scale(size / 25) {
  for(j = [0, 1]) mirror([j, 0, 0]) for(i = [for(i = [0:10]) i / 10])
translate([0, pow(i, 2) * 10, 0])
    rotate(180 * sqrt(i)) hull() {
      scale([.1, pow(i, .5) * 10]) rotate(-135) square();
      circle(pow((i + 1), 1) * .5);
    }
  hull() for(j = [0, 1]) mirror([j, 0, 0]) for(i = [for(i = [0:10])
  i / 10]) translate([0, pow(i, 2) * 10, 0])
    rotate(180 * sqrt(i)) circle(pow((i + 1), 1) * .5);
}
```

```
linear_extrude(hole * 2, convexity = 5) difference() {
  circle((hole/2 + 1.2) / cos(180 / 8), $fn = 8);
  circle((hole/2) / cos(180 / 8), $fn = 8);
}
```

Printing Suggestions

Some of the models in this chapter may require support, as mentioned. MatterControl generates support automatically if you tell it to (see Appendix A). Generally speaking, if a petal or leaf is hanging out in the breeze and is significantly flatter than a 45-degree angle to the platform, you probably need support. The daisy was this way; the camellia was printable without support. If the contact area with the platform is small, you may also want to use a raft, as described in Appendix A.

If you want to test whether or not your outer petals will need support, you can increase the petalOffset value to be equal to the value you plan to use plus two or three less than your total planned petals. For instance, we tested a three-petal camellia to see if we could print it without support. The full camellia has petals = 89 and petalOffset = 21; we ran a test with petals = 3 and petalOffset = 21 + 89 - 3 = 107. This allowed us to see with a 3-petal version whether we could get away with doing the rather lengthy camellia print without support. (The answer was we could—see Figure 6-15 for the test print.)

Figure 6-15. *Testing a "partial camellia"*

■ **Tip**   Some of these models take quite a long time to render in OpenSCAD and MatterControl. They may also take a while to print; the models we show in this chapter each took many hours on our relatively fast, small Bukito printers. Plan ahead if you want to use them in a class.

THINKING ABOUT THE MODELS: LEARNING LIKE A MAKER

This chapter started with the idea that it would be interesting to see how well the math described earlier in this chapter would actually create plants with plausible-looking (or at least plausibly-functioning) structures for different environments. Fairly rapidly, though, we needed to go out and look at as many plants as we could to see how the plants handled things like overlapping leaves and petals, and how real plants attached and added on structure. At some point Rich realized that he could adapt the techniques used to describe the shape of an airfoil from Chapter 4 to create petal/leaf individual objects. That plus the basic spiral distribution got us underway.

Showing plants for wet and dry environments seemed like a good way to showcase two opposite ecosystem types. However, we realized early on that a desert plant for the most part is a pretty natural match to 3D printing. Many desert plants have structures that point straight up or gradually bend inward from a broad base, since the plants tend to want to encourage water runoff right to their small root systems. This makes them relatively easy to capture in a 3D print.

Similarly, the basic flower blooms we were modeling could be delicate prints, but could be printed flat and with no or minimal support just from the platform. (There are, of course, many flower blooms that were not really feasible on a consumer-level printer, but the ones here will let you think about the issues of attracting pollinators in different environments.)

Jungle plants, with their arched leaves and suspended airy leaves, were a different story. To maintain the water-shedding arched shapes of many leaves in these environments, we printed out leaves individually and put them into a base that spaces them in an Archimedes spiral. We decided against modeling any particular plant leaf in detail, but instead focused on the sparse foliage and water-shedding structure of the plants like calla lilies and philodendrons.

Briefly we thought about trying to model the process plants use to add a leaf or petal more accurately, but decided that just empirically creating a model that gave a physical model at the end which got some big-picture features right was more flexible and more broadly applicable—not wanting to lose sight of the forest for the trees, as it were. Since the models are very nonlinear and the parameters to allow for a lot of shapes can result in some interesting interactions, we encourage you to play with "evolving" some cool species (by changing model variables) and think about where they might flourish in the real world.

Where to Learn More

There are a lot of good botany books aimed at the general public. Many are aimed at gardeners, such as Brian Capon's books *Botany for Gardeners* (Revised edition, Timber Press, 2005) and *Plant Survival: Adapting to a Hostile World* (Timber Press, 1994). As the titles would imply, the first one is a general introduction to how plants make a living, whereas the second is a great survey of how a plant and its ecosystem interact.

One book that was particular helpful in thinking about creating these models was Lizabeth Leech's book *Botany for Artists* (The Crowood Press, 2011), which had many wonderful structural discussions and deconstructions about how to think about and represent plant structure. If you want to do more artistically sophisticated 3D models than the ones shown in this chapter, you might find Leech's book very helpful both in how to look at and analyze a plant's structure, and also for the many very detailed, clear pictures and diagrams of plants.

To learn more about extinction in a rapidly changing world, Elizabeth Kolbert's Pulitzer-Prize-winning book *The Sixth Extinction* (Picador, 2015) is a good general-public review of the issues and the people trying to understand them.

If you would like to do chemistry experiments with plants and understand the science behind their coloration, David Lee's book *Nature's Palette: The Science of Plant Color* (University of Chicago Press, 2007) has some great experiments with basic hardware-store materials that might be interesting for a lab course.

We have given some references for the mathematics of the golden ratio and the Fibonacci sequence where we introduced the topic. The Khan Academy (www.khanacademy.org) has many great videos on the math and also on the places where the ratios occur in nature and architecture. Search on *golden ratio* and *Fibonacci*.

If you live near a major botanical garden, or can take a virtual tour of one, nothing compares to seeing plant communities in the wild. We highly recommend seeing some full-scale, real ecosystems before trying to design your own.

Teacher Tips

As noted earlier, we could imagine these models being used just as literal plants to play with in the K–2 grades. See the K–2 science standards about interrelationships between plants, animals, and where they live, such as K-ESS3-1 at www.nextgenscience.org/topic-arrangement/kinterdependent-relationships-ecosystems-animals-plants-and-their-environment.

In middle school, standards such as MS-LS2-5 may apply—see www.nextgenscience.org/pe/ms-ls2-5-ecosystems-interactions-energy-and-dynamics.

In high school, these models might find a use teaching standards such as HS-LS2-7, designing solutions to reduce human impacts on biodiversity (www.nextgenscience.org/pe/hs-ls2-7-ecosystems-interactions-energy-and-dynamics).

These are just a few topics that struck us as interesting tie-ins to add the concept of considering what plant features would make the plant more likely to survive in a given ecosystem. We are sure that teachers will come up with better ones based on your experiences.

If this exercise inspires you to go out and observe plants in the wild, you can help with a citizen science project and gather data. If you browse projects on www.inaturalist.org, you can probably find a botanical project near you where you and your students can contribute observations.

Science Fair Project Ideas

You can build a science fair project around these models in several directions. First you could simply try changing the different variables in the models and seeing what sort of plants you get based on the mathematics and compare them to real plants. Do real flowers with thin, widely separated petals tend to always have 3, 5, or 8 petals, for instance? How often do plants fit the rule? Do plants of a species always have the same number of petals?

Alternatively, you could start with a rule, like *I am going to design a garden for a very sunny, hot, dry climate*. How would you shape the plants—and mix them into a community—to use the available sun, manage excess sun, and use water well? What does your community look like? Does it look like real desert plant communities? How would your plant community fare if the climate changed suddenly? Analyzing the differences in real plant communities and your constructed ones might lead you to some interesting explorations of climate, evolution, and mutations.

You might also consider what would happen if you inserted an "invasive species" into your carefully balanced plant grouping. What might it displace? What else might happen to the other organisms (bugs, microbes, and so on) in the ecosystem? Where do they live? You could also imagine creating a game that would track which plants got enough (or too much) water, sun, or nutrients to see which species might be the winners and losers in the presence of an invasive species.

Summary

In this chapter, you learned about different types of plants and how they have evolved structures that make them successful in their environments. We developed some simple ways to create notional models of plants, and explored how one might use these models to think about plants and their roles in their ecosystems.

CHAPTER 7

■■■

Molecules

A lot of the art of chemistry involves being able to visualize abstract descriptions of activities that are occurring on the atomic or molecular level. Often these abstractions can be described mathematically with very complex equations that most people will not see until later years in college, if then. In this chapter we show you how to create a few minimalist models that may help you develop intuition about these interactions.

Chemistry books usually are pretty dense with diagrams and equations. As a conscious departure from that, we illustrate the concepts in this chapter with photographs of the models themselves so that you can see how the explanation and the model go together.

First we give you some chemistry background and explain terminology for our models. Then we talk about how we came up with these models and how we think you might use them to teach or learn the concepts embodied in them, and perhaps how to extend the models for your own uses or science projects. Rather than create a giant set of models that captures many circumstances, we have stuck to just two: a carbon atom and a water molecule. Then we look at how these atoms are incorporated into crystals.

Joan and Rich would like to thank Michael Cheverie, a teacher of the visually impaired in Los Angeles who initially suggested using 3D-printed models to teach organic chemistry to blind students. Mike then worked with us to define the carbon models and contributed to some of the chemistry background and teacher exercises that we have incorporated into this chapter. Glaciologist Frank Carsey was kind enough to read our discussion of ice.

Chemistry Background

Atoms form chemical *bonds* with one another through an interaction between their *electrons*. In this way molecules are created out of atoms. Electrons are very tiny particles with a negative electric charge that whir around the positively charged, relatively large nucleus of the atom. About 100 years ago, physicist Niels Bohr proposed that the electrons orbit the nucleus in much the same way as planets orbit a star in a solar system. This is good for visualizing a very rough model of an atom, but the reality is more complicated than that and rapidly gets in to the realm of quantum mechanics.

You can buy kits of varying levels of sophistication to create physical models of chemical bond structure. Most of them fall into two categories: either very simple models of the basic shapes of the "clouds" of electrons that interact with other atoms to form molecules, or "ball and stick" models of how atoms go together to create molecules. Both have their good points and shortcomings, and in this chapter we talk about our process of coming up with a few minimalist models that you can use as the basis of your own explorations.

Valence Electrons and the Periodic Table

Chemistry can seem like a maze of unconnected facts to memorize that have no guiding principles to hang them all together. However, the *periodic table of the elements* (see sidebar) gives us some rules and organization about how atoms are constructed and how they come together with other atoms.

Only electrons that are the farthest from the nucleus of the atom are involved in bonding atoms to one another. These are called *valence electrons*. Atoms can share one or more valence electrons with other atoms, forming a chemical bond known as a *covalent bond*. Groups of atoms that are covalently bonded to one another are known as *molecules*.

Molecules have different properties than do the individual atoms that make them up. Whether an atom of a representative element will bond with another, and how it will bond, depends not just on the number of valence electrons the atom has but also on how many fewer than eight valence electrons it has. Atoms of the representative elements can have at most eight valence electrons. If an atom has fewer than eight valence electrons, then it will bond with other atoms so that it can obtain a full set of eight valence electrons through sharing electrons with the other atoms. (This is called the *octet rule*. A full octet consists of eight electrons.)

Some atoms have a full octet of eight valence electrons. These atoms will not bond with others under any sort of normal circumstance. Thus these elements are called the *noble gases* since they are sort of above interacting with any other, mere peasant substance, and because they are all gases at Earth temperature and pressures. All the atoms of the other representative elements are lacking a full octet, so they form covalent bonds with other atoms to get their full octet. Bonding ultimately creates all the chemical compounds in existence.

THE PERIODIC TABLE OF THE ELEMENTS

The *periodic table of the elements* is a classic depiction showing the relationships between different atoms in a compact graphical way. The elements are arranged into 18 columns, called *groups*, and 7 rows (called *periods*). There is also another set of "series" of elements that fall outside this charactization.

A tremendous amount of information is embodied in the periodic table, and some nuances may be important if you decide to do an independent project in this area. Rather than capture a subset of it here, we suggest you look at one of the many good online versions of the periodic table. (Just search on *periodic table*.)

We particularly like https://en.wikipedia.org/wiki/Periodic_table and www.rsc.org/periodic-table (which includes podcasts and many links from Britain's Royal Society of Chemistry). The elements in groups (columns) 1, 2, and 13–18 of the periodic table are called the *representative elements*. The electron structures of the atoms of these elements give them a great deal of flexibility in forming *chemical bonds* with atoms of other elements.

The number of valence electrons an atom has can be determined by looking at its position in the periodic table. Atoms of the elements in periodic table group 1 have one valence electron. Elements in group 2 have two valence electrons. The elements in groups 13 through 18 follow this pattern with a twist: group 13 elements have 3 valence electrons, and so on up through group 18—elements with 8 valence electrons. An atom's overall number of electrons is equal to its *atomic number*.

Basic Orbital Shapes

Atoms are made up of clouds of electrons that take on a particular shape, depending on a lot of things that we will talk about next. The Schrödinger equation (http://en.wikipedia.org/wiki/Schr%C3%B6dinger_equation) describes how electrons behave in an atom. This equation results in solutions that tell us that electrons like to fly in certain particular regions of space called *electron clouds*, or *probability clouds*—regions where the probability of finding an electron is high. An analogy is a swarm of gnats; any given spot may not have a gnat in it at any time, but the swarm appears to have a shape from a distance. Dealing with general solutions to Schrödinger's equation, though, is usually a graduate-school activity. Below that level, usually the shapes that these clouds make are just shown as something to memorize. These clouds are made up of *orbitals*—particular regions where electrons are likely to be found (https://en.wikipedia.org/wiki/Atomic_orbital).

In the case of a carbon atom (one of the representative elements, with six valence electrons), there are two fundamental shapes of these orbitals. Sometimes they are described as four types of orbitals because one type can be oriented one of three mutually perpendicular ways. The simplest one is the spherical *s* orbital, and the one with three possible orientations is the dumbbell-shaped *p* orbital. The arrangement of the *s* and *p* orbitals for a carbon atom is shown in Figure 7-1. The *s* orbital is blue, and the *p* orbitals, grey.

Figure 7-1. *A carbon atom's nucleus (mostly hidden by s orbital), s and p orbitals. The "real" s orbital is a complete sphere; the holes here are to make it possible to assemble a solid-object representation*

Carbon Atom Model

The carbon atom model consists of a nucleus, two *s* orbital halves (which snap together), and three *p* orbital pieces, as you can see in Figure 7-2. Note that the sphere-shaped *s* orbital is at the center of the arrangement (surrounding the nucleus). The three *p* orbitals intersect the *s* orbital and are perpendicular to one another. Chemists label these *p* orbitals as p_x, p_y, and p_z where *x*, *y*, and *z* stand for the axes in a 3-dimensional coordinate system. Since the shapes are identical and only different in orientation, we have created just one model that you can place in the three orientations.

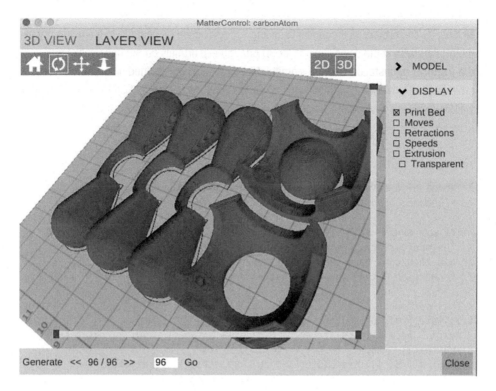

Figure 7-2. *The carbon atom parts, printing all at once*

Each of the orbitals, s, p_x, p_y, and p_z, can hold a maximum of two electrons. In *quantum mechanics* (the study of how things at this scale behave), each electron is designated by a set of numbers called *quantum numbers,* sort of an identifier for that electron in that molecule. Any given electron in an atom has to have a unique set of quantum numbers. Two electrons that are in the same orbital, say the p_x orbital, differ only in their spin (called by convention *spin up* or *spin down,* an abstract concept that has nothing to do with direction of gravity).

Printing the Carbon Atom

The model in Listing 7-1 prints out all the pieces at once. Figure 7-2 shows the layout of the model in MatterControl. Listing 7-1 creates models for the nucleus, *s* orbital halves, and *p* orbitals. If you wanted to print out the molecule in more than one color (as we show here), you could print two in different colors and mix and match (probably the easiest approach). Alternatively, see the comments in the listing about which part to comment out to just print some of the parts each time.

■ **Note** The orbitals in the model in Listing 7-1 are based on best fits to the geometry of the orbitals with some compromises for 3D printing—*p* orbitals do not have hooks around the *s* orbital, for instance, and the *s* orbital does not have well-defined holes in it for the *p* orbitals. They are not fundametal solutions of the wave equations that underly them. In other words, these are designed to "look right" rather than derived from physics.

Listing 7-1. Carbon Atom Model

```
// Model of a carbon atom - nucleus and s and p orbitals
// Filename: carbonAtom.scad

// If you want to make one of the pieces a different color, you can comment out
// the appropriate line of the next three, generate an STL,
// and then come back and comment out the OTHER two lines
// to make an STL of the other parts

//This section creates the p orbitals, s orbitals, and nucleus for printing
translate([-41, 0, 0]) {
  for(i = [0:2]) translate([0, i * 22, 5]) rotate([0, 90, ]) rotate(-16)
p_orbital();
  for(i = [-1, 1]) translate([i * 20, -30, 17.5]) s_orbital();
  translate([20, -30, 10 * (sin(52.5))]) nucleus();
}

$fs = 2;
$fa = 2;

//This section displays the p orbitals, s orbitals, and nucleus to show how
// they are assembled
//% modifier means they will not be included when rendering
%translate([41, 0, 0]) {
  nucleus();
  for(l = [0, 1]) rotate([180 * l, 0, 0]) s_orbital();
  for(i = [0:2]) rotate([i ? 90 : 0, i ? ((i == 1) ? 45 : 135) : 0, i ?
  ((i == 1) ? 0 : -90) : 45])
    p_orbital();
}
```

```
//create the nucleus (sphere with a flat side for printing)
module nucleus() scale(1.0) difference() {
  sphere(10);
  translate([0, 0, -10 * (1 + sin(52.5))]) cube(20, center = true);
}

//create s orbital halves
module s_orbital() difference() {
  sphere(22);
  sphere(18);
  for(i = [-1:1]) rotate([0, 90 * i, 45 * i + 45]) {
    cylinder(r = 10.5, h = 100, center = true);
    for(j = [-1, 1]) translate([0, 0, j * (50 + 17.5)]) cube(100, center = true);
  }
  translate([0, 0, 50 + 2]) cube(100, center = true);
  intersection() {
    union() {
      rotate([90, 0, 45]) linear_extrude(100, center = true, convexity = 5)
      for(m = [0, 1])
        mirror([m, 0, 0]) translate([20, 0, 0]) rotate(-5)
        translate([0, -3, 0]) square(10);
      rotate([90, 0, -45]) linear_extrude(100, center = true,
      convexity = 5) for(m = [0, 1])
        mirror([m, 0, 0]) translate([20, 0, 0]) rotate(5 + 180)
        translate([0, -3, 0]) square(10);
    }
    translate([0, 0, 50 - 2]) cube(100, center = true);
  }
}

//create p orbital lobes
module p_orbital() difference() {
  union() {
    for(i = [1, -1]) hull() {
      sphere(2);
      translate([0, 0, i * 30]) sphere(10);
    }
    intersection() {
      sphere(12);
      linear_extrude(height = 100, center = true) hull() for(j = [0, 1])
translate([0, j * 15, 0])
        circle(5 - 4 * j);
    }
  }
```

```
for(i = [1, -1]) rotate([-90, 0, i * 45]) hull() {
  sphere(1);
  translate([0, 0, 30]) sphere(10);
}
sphere(10);
rotate(16) translate([55, 0, 0]) cube(100, center = true);
}
```

How to Assemble the Carbon Atom Model

These models can be a little tricky to assemble the first time. First, take the nucleus and wrap the *p* orbitals around it. The *p* orbitals are designed so that their connectors will not cross each other on the nucleus (Figure 7-3).

Figure 7-3. *Assembling the carbon atom nucleus and p orbitals*

Next, take the *s* orbital halves and arrange the *p* orbitals so that they are sticking out the holes in the *s* orbital halves. You will see that there are slight indentations on the outside of two of the arms of the *s* orbital halves, and on the inside of the other two. Line up the halves so that the arms that have indentations on the outside hook into arms that have them on the inside (Figure 7-4). Squeeze the arms that will be inside a little to make the model pop together. You can see the final version back in Figure 7-1.

Figure 7-4. *Adding the s orbital to the carbon atom*

■ **Note**   In this chapter, we occasionally use chemical formula notation, which consists of the letters for each atom from the periodic table (for example, C for carbon) and a subscript that says how many of that atom is in the particular molecule. So C_2H_6 has two carbon atoms and six hydrogen (H) ones.

WHEN ATOMS BOND TOGETHER: HYBRIDIZATION

The orbitals described in the preceding section are a fleeting thing if other atoms are around. When atoms get together, attractive and repulsive forces among the electron clouds result in a new steady state. This adjustment is called *hybridization.* This process affects the geometry of the resulting molecules. That geometry in large part determines the chemical properties of the molecule.

Hybridization occurs only with orbitals that contain valence electrons. The *s* orbital of an atom combines with one or more of the *p* orbitals to form a new orbital structure, a *hybridized orbital.* After hybridization, the (hybridized) orbitals of the atom will contain at least one electron, but at most two electrons. Each of the hybridized orbitals that contain one electron can share that one electron with a similar hybridized orbital containing one electron in another atom. Thus, the two atoms are able to share two electrons between them, thereby forming a *covalent bond.*

141

There can be three types of hybrid orbital: sp^1 (usually written just sp), sp^2, and sp^3. The superscript denotes how many p orbitals have been combined with the s orbital. The discussion in this sidebar about each of these applies to *carbon atoms* and their compounds. Hybridization of other atoms, like nitrogen and oxygen, are a little different. We talk very broadly about what happens in water ice later on.

sp^3 Hybridization

An atom that is sp^3-hybridized has combined its s orbital and all three p orbitals to make four sp^3-hybridized orbitals, each one with large lobe and one small one. Orbitals do not lie in the same plane; an angle of 109.5 degrees exists between each of the lobes in sp^3-hybridization, creating tetrahedral structures. To create a methane molecule, for example, a single electron in each lobe can form a single bond with a hydrogen atom.

This type of bond between hybridized orbitals is called a *sigma (σ) bond*. It is formed between the orbitals of two atoms along a straight line that joins the nuclei of the two atoms. The single electrons that are in the small lobes of the sp-hybridized orbitals are not between the two atoms, but are on the *outside*, where they can bond with other atoms.

This is the type of bond that appears in diamond and water ice crystals, which we talk about in the next section.

sp^2 Hybridization

A second type of hybridization is called sp^2 *hybridization*. An atom that is sp^2-*hybridized* hybridized has combined its s orbital with two of its p orbitals. Ethene (C_2H_4) is an example of a molecule in which a carbon atom is sp^2-hybridized.

sp Hybridization

The final type of hybridization is called *sp-hybridization*. In sp-hybridization, one of the p orbitals combines with the s orbital to make two sp-hybridized orbitals, while leaving the two remaining p orbitals unchanged. The sp-hybridized orbitals align on the same axis as each other, facing opposite directions. Ethyne (C_2H_2) has two sp-hybridized carbon atoms bonded with one another.

Water Molecules

A water molecule consists of two hydrogen atoms bonded to one oxygen atom. Hydrogen bonds tend to be dynamic, and the hydrogen atom bonds to one oxygen atom covalently, but also wants to bond with nearby other oxygen atoms too. Water has some pretty weird properties, chemically speaking—its boiling point is much higher than one would expect, for example, and it is denser as a liquid than it is as a solid (ice). Most of these properties are thought to come from these hydrogen bonds.

Oxygen has six valence electrons. In a water molecule, two hydrogen atoms each bond with one of the oxygen atoms' valence electrons. This leaves two pairs of electrons on the oxygen molecule. The two hydrogens are sort of squished over to one side of the atom by these free pairs, so that the atom is close to being part of a tetrahedron.

The Water Molecule Model

We have modeled one water molecule as an oxygen atom with two attached hydrogens and two "holes" (the other oxygen electron pairs) which the hydrogens of other molecules can then connect to. For 3D-printing convenience, we have printed our molecules in halves, with a flat side (Figure 7-5). If you wanted just one water molecule, you could glue these together. But these were really designed to put into models of solid water—the crystalline structure we know as ice.

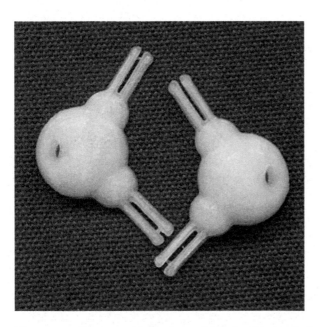

Figure 7-5. Our water molecule model (printed in two halves)

A water molecule's hydrogens are not quite at the points of a tetrahedron; they are slightly less (about 104.5 degrees, versus 109.5 for a tetrahedron). We have made the hydrogen's bond that wants to connect to another oxygen a pair of thin plug connectors so that they will flex a bit when we create a structure from them. Listing 7-2 is the OpenSCAD model for these molecules.

Listing 7-2. The Water Molecule

```
//Model to create a water molecule with connectors
// To create an ice lattice
// File water.scad
Od = 20;  //Oxygen atom diameter, mm
Hd = 10;  //Hydrogen atom diamter, mm
OHspacing = 10;  //Offset between centers of O and H atoms, mm
peg = 5; //diameter of the peg , mm
tol = .2;    //Tolerance (empty space) between peg in hole and peg
peg_len = 10; // length of the peg

$fs = .5;
$fa = 2;

//pick angle of the structure; last one shown will be used by program
angle = acos(-1/3); //tetrahedral, ~109.5
angle = 104.5; //water

for(a = [0, 180]) rotate(a) translate([-9, 12.5, 0,]) rotate(angle / 2 - 90)
half();

//Now create the half a moledule
module half() difference() {
  union() {
    sphere(Od/2);
    for(i = [-1, 1]) rotate(angle/2 * i) {
      translate([OHspacing, 0, 0]) sphere(Hd/2);
      rotate([0, 90, 0]) difference() {
        union() {
          cylinder(r = peg / 2, h = OHspacing + Hd/2 + peg_len);
          scale([5/6, 1, 1]) translate([0, 0, OHspacing + Hd/2 + peg_len])
hull()
            rotate_extrude(convexity = 5) translate([-peg / 3, 0, 0])
circle(peg / 4);
        }
        cube([peg * 2, peg/4, (OHspacing + Hd/2 + peg_len) * 3],
        center = true);
      }
    }
  }
}
```

```
    for(i = [-1, 1]) rotate([0, angle/2 * i - 90, 0])
      translate([0, 0, (peg + tol) * sin(angle) / 2 + (peg + tol)/4])
        rotate_extrude(convexity = 5) {
          hull() {
            translate([peg / 2, 0, 0]) circle(peg / 4 + tol);
            translate([0, -peg/4 - tol, 0]) square([tol, peg / 2 + tol * 2]);
          }
          square([peg / 2 + tol, 0d]);
        }
    translate([0, 0, -100 + tol/2]) cube(200, center = true);
}
```

The Carbon vs. Water Molecule Model

You will notice that in the case of the carbon atom, we showed it as having six lobes that "stuck out" to show its orbitals. This model, obviously, cannot then be used to construct other models by putting together carbon atoms, since there are no ways to hook them together. The carbon atom model was purely an exercise in showing the orbitals. The water molecule model, however, has two plugs that stick out (showing the attached hydrogen atoms) and two holes that can be filled by those plugs. Really, both carbon atoms and the water molecules like to make four connections. However, this is tricky to make in a replicable model. The water molecule is made this way to point out the two types of hydrogen bond it can make, but you should keep in mind that it is an abstraction.

Crystals

When many substances become solid, they form a *crystal*—a regular, repeating pattern of molecules. In this section, we look at two crystals that form based on their sp^3 bonds—two kinds of water ice—and talk about similarities to diamond, which is a crystal form of carbon.

Crystals are made up of *base cells*—sets of atoms in a particular pattern that repeat over and over—in a structure called a *lattice*. For 3D printing, we find the concept of a base cell less than useful, since the cells are designed to be grasped from a 2D drawing. When you can work freely in 3D, other structures are more natural, and we discuss those emergent structures here.

The water molecule model in Listing 7-2 creates just one "pair of halves" of a water molecule. In Figure 7-6, we show how we printed nine molecules at a time. (See Appendix A for information on how to use OpenSCAD and MatterControl and for some brief instructions about 3D printing in general.) Now we will take a large number of these molecules and see what kind of structures we can create.

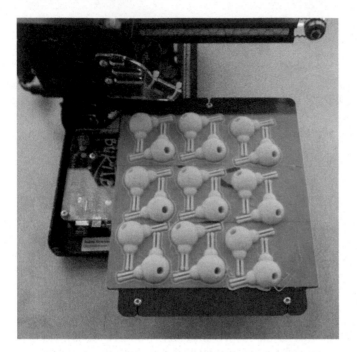

Figure 7-6. *Nine water molecule models printed at once*

Water Ice

When water is above its freezing temperature, it flows freely. Water molecules transiently "stick to" each other as the hydrogen electrons (the plugs, on our models) come under the influence of the free pairs of electrons on other oxygen atoms (the holes, in our models). However, when the water is cooled enough, order begins to evolve from this chaos, and a crystalline form—ice—begins to form.

Depending on the circumstances, water ice can form in one of several different crystal structures; there is a good review at https://en.wikipedia.org/wiki/Ice. In this section, we talk about two lattice structures: ice 1h and ice 1c. Both are formed fundamentally of tetrahedrons (they use the *sp³* bonding covered in the sidebar about hybridization earlier in the chapter.) But you will see that small differences in how the molecules connect can lead to some big structural differences.

Ice 1h

The commonest ice structure at temperatures and pressures normally encountered on the surface of the Earth is called *ice 1h*. It consists of layers of hexagons, with the layers regularly lined up one under the other. This is shown in Figures 7-7 through 7-9. (*Top* and *side* are arbitrary here, meant to show views taken at right angles from each other.)

146

■ **Note**   You can see from Figures 7-7 through 7-9 that the water molecules in ice are quite sparsely packed into the space. This is the reason that ice is less dense than liquid water. If that were not true, then ice would sink to the bottom of lakes in winter and keep refreezing at the top until the whole lake was frozen. This would be very bad for any fish in a lake that freezes over in winter, since the layer of unfrozen water at the bottom of a frozen lake is habitat for many species, entirely dependent on this property.

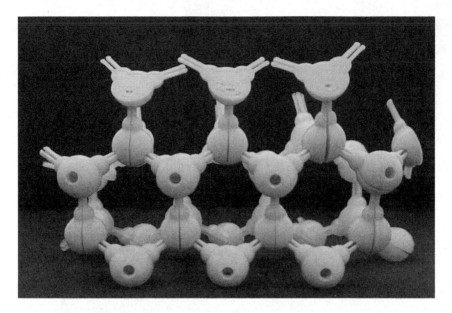

Figure 7-7. *Ice 1h (hexagonal) model, bottom view*

Figure 7-8. *Ice 1h model, side view*

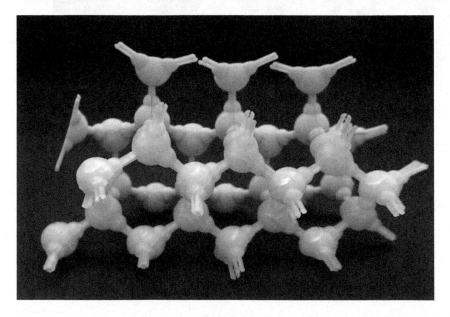

Figure 7-9. *Ice 1h model, top view. The hexagons line up (shown at slight offset angle from straight down so that the lower row is visible)*

Assembling an Ice 1h Molecule

Assembling the models is a little tricker than it looks. We recommend that you create the pattern apparent in the blue "bottom layer" of Figure 7-7 first and then build up from it. Alternate having the spikes stick up (and thus have a hole on the bottom) and having them stick out sideways to connect two molecules. Figure 7-7 plus the side and top views in Figures 7-8 and 7-9 should be helpful.

■ **Note** The structure will go together in various ways that are "legal" (a peg in a hole), so you have to be careful about creating your pattern consistently. This is physical; ice usually has irregularities in its crystal structure. We are showing two different ideal structures in this chapter. Joan found it easiest to think about the molecules in a layer having the bond alternately sticking up and sideways from one model to the next.

There is no particular reason why we have alternating layers different colors—we just wanted you to be able to see how they go together. We have "half molecules" holding the molecules along the edges together, since the two halves of each water molecule do not otherwise stick. You could glue the halves together ahead of time, but that is not really necessary. The "half molecules" help show how the structure would continue anyway. You can print as many molecules as will fit on your print bed; you need quite a few to make a model.

You will probably discover that you need to hold the two halves together with one hand, and the rest of the structure with the other. You might want to have the three views of the model in front of you as you lay out the first layer.

■ **Tip** If you print these molecules in PLA, you may want to avoid leaving them lying about assembled, particularly in a warm environment like a parked car. There is a bit of spring force in the parts holding them together, but PLA will creep to relieve this stress, particularly in a warm environment.

Ice 1c

Another form of water ice, *ice 1c* (for more, see https://en.wikipedia.org/wiki/Ice_Ic), is a body-centered cubic crystal lattice structure. Compared to ice 1h, it is a differently arranged repeating set of tetrahedrons. Each row is offset from the next, as shown in the bottom view of Figure 7-10 (equivalent to the view in Figure 7-7 for ice 1h). If we had a third layer on top of the white one, it would line up with the blue one, and so on. On Earth, ice 1c is found in high clouds (like cirrus clouds) where the water is supercooled before ice crystals form—that is, the water in the cloud is below the freezing point for that pressure and temperature.

Figures 7-11 and 7-12 show this structure from the side and the top, equivalent to Figures 7-9 and 7-10 for ice 1h. You can see that now the hexagons are offset from layer to layer versus lying directly above one another, as they did in ice 1h (Figure 7-8).

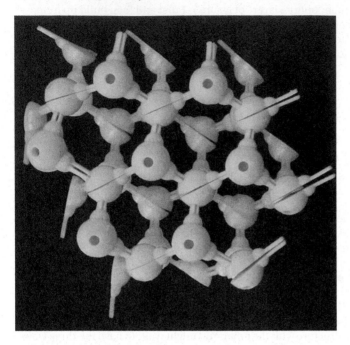

Figure 7-10. *Ice 1c model, bottom view*

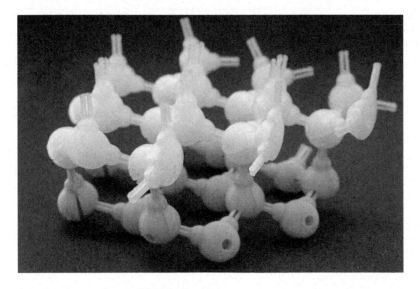

Figure 7-11. *Ice 1c model, side view*

150

Figure 7-12. *Ice 1c model, top view*

Assembling the Ice 1c Molecule

Assembling the ice 1c molecule is similar to the ice 1h. Take a careful look at the three pictures of the structure, and build the bottom layer bearing in mind how the molecules alternate in their up/down patterns. The ice 1c model was built out from a central first hexagon as a somewhat more natural way to lay out this structure, versus laying out several rows, as was done with the ice 1h.

Other Water Ice Structures

Water ice forms other crystal structures at low temperatures and high pressures that are created in a lab, or possibly are found on other planets. These are described with numbers (ices II–XII) and most of them are not very stable. Fortunately, Kurt Vonnegut's incredibly destructive *ice-nine* (in his novel *Cat's Cradle*) is fictional. The late Barclay Kamb at Caltech did a lot of interesting work in this area; if you want to learn more, you might start by looking up some of his papers in library databases that carry scientific journals, or at http://scholar.google.com). Or you can search on each of the types, like the very unstable *ice IV.*

Diamond

As it happens, ice 1c and diamonds (crystalline carbon) have very similar structures. A carbon atom can bond to four other carbon atoms in a tetrahedron—this happens in diamond—and also with bonds to four hydrogen atoms to create methane.

If you ignore the "hydrogen atom" bumps on our ice 1c structure, and the fact that the angle between the plugs there is 104.5 degrees instead of the true tetrahedral 109 degrees, the ice 1c model is a pretty good representation of diamond. Diamonds are so incredibly strong in part because each carbon atom is connected to four other ones in roughly the same configuration as ice 1c.

If the carbon atoms instead were strongly bonded to three others in a flat sheet, and then weakly bonded between sheets, we would instead get graphite (the "lead" in pencils). If you had a structure like just one layer of ice 1c (or, for that matter, ice 1h since the single layers are the same) and allowed those to be loosely connected, you get the structure of graphite. Graphite is conductive because it has those extra electrons only loosely bonded, and is weak because these layers can slide over each other.

THINKING ABOUT THESE MODELS: LEARNING LIKE A MAKER

Neither of us had taken chemistry for quite some time and so essentially had to re-learn the material to create these models. When we started researching it in earnest, we were struck by how most texts and lectures spent a very long time on nomenclature and orbitals that actually are not present in most compounds, but are precursors to ones that are. Chemistry teacher Michael Cheverie (acknowledged at more length at the beginning of this chapter) spent a lot of time with us reminding us about the details.

However, we were overwhelmed in structural detail and trying to create a general set of models that would work for a variety of molecules. Nothing clicked until we reminded ourselves of the maker dictum: find a moderately complex example, build it, and pick up the basics as you go. Then, use that as a base to learn more complex cases.

Our first attempt was to model a methane molecule: one carbon atom and four hydrogens. We came to it by sketching, using all four of our hands to hold things in place, and pestering chemist friends for physical details. At the end, we had a pretty good understanding of the chemistry and felt like we validated learning by making in the process. But then we decided that even this simple carbon model was too sophisticated relative to the level of the rest of the models in the book, and we decided to back off to just the few interesting lattices we ultimately included.

Physical model design requires some compromises. Since we are modeling something that is not a physical solid but rather clouds of electrons, of necessity there are some constraints required to make it possible to have the models work mechanically. We have tried to minimize those constraints but could not eliminate them. In particular, to make the models easier to 3D print, parts have a strategic flat spot or two that make the models a little different than common rounded representations of these electron clouds.

We found that the constraints of making something easy to print and easy to assemble and accurate were overwhelming if one wanted to allow the user to "completely dissassemble" a model of a substance like diamond or ice down to its electron orbitals. Thus we came to the whole-molecule-level crystal element models that appear in the chapter.

Printing Suggestions

The models in this chapter are a little trickier to print and assemble than some of those in earlier chapters. Here are some rules of thumb:

- Do not scale these models up or down (particularly not down). The were created with wall thicknesses that were designed to be a little springy (which will not work if they get much thicker) or with parts that will get too thin and small to print reliably if you make them smaller. You may need to change the models a bit if you want a bigger or smaller one.

- The water molecule halves are rather delicate and tend to fly off the platform when you use a tool to spatula them off the build platform.

- Treat the water molecule halves as science learning tools and not general construction toys—the parts are small and could be younger-sibling choking hazards.

- If your platform is not perfectly aligned you may want to print with a raft to ensure clean mating surfaces. See the Appendix A discussion on this and similar issues.

Where to Learn More

There are many books and websites devoted to explaining the topics in this chapter. We referred often to Gary L. Miessler and Donald A. Tarr's text *Organic Chemistry,* 2nd Edition (Prentice Hall, 2000), to remind us of all that general chemistry background we learned once and had since forgotten. We have relegated most of the chemical bonding detail to a sidebar, but if you want to learn more about that in particular, here are some resources that we particularly liked:

- The Khan Academy has many great videos on chemistry fundamentals. Their tutorials in the section "Hybridization and Hybrid Orbitals" are particularly helpful: www.khanacademy.org/ science/chemistry/chemical-bonds/copy-of-covalent-bonds.

- This site has excellent pictures and explanations: http:// chemwiki.ucdavis.edu/Theoretical_Chemistry/Chemical_ Bonding/Valence_Bond_Theory.

- This one has good diagrams and tables that give examples of molecule geometries resulting from different types of bonds: www.kidzsearch.com/wiki/Orbital_hybridization.

- This video explains hybridization in terms of energy: www.youtube.com/watch?v=HKyobMewXBw.

- These videos use balloons to model bonding—it becomes clear pretty quickly why 3D printing is a bit more manageable way to go, but the visualization is fun: www.youtube. com/watch?v=bOKvfvJi-vk and www.youtube.com/ watch?v=KbOmxAMHnfE.

To learn about water and ice, we used the Wikipedia pages linked in those sections, as wells as the results of and general searches online for *ice cubic lattice* and *ice hexagonal.* We also enjoyed dipping around in Mariana Gosnell's book *Ice: The Nature, the History, and the Uses of an Astonishing Substance* (Alfred A. Knopf, 2005).

The website http://www1.lsbu.ac.uk/water/ also has a great deal of well-organized information for further exploration. The Khan Academy has this: www. khanacademy.org/science/biology/water-acids-and-bases/water-as-a-solid-liquid-and-gas/v/liquid-water-denser-than-solid-water-ice.

To learn about diamonds, besides the results of online searches on *diamond crystal structure,* we used Eric Bruton's *Diamonds,* 2nd edition (Chilton Book Company, 1978).

Teacher Tips

We have looked at the Next Generation Science Standards to see where the models in this chapter might most usefully fit into a curriculum. You should look at your own state and school's requirements and come up with your own best alignments. It seemed to us that the best fit might be within units covering these standards:

- HS-PS1: Chemical Reactions www.nextgenscience.org/topic-arrangement/hschemical-reactions

- PS-1 Matter and its Interactions: www.nextgenscience.org/dci-arrangement/ms-ps1-matter-and-its-interactions

Science Fair Project Ideas

These models are useful as-is to learn chemistry and to think about chemical bonding. Thus, the first "experiment" to do with them is simply to print them out and see how they fit together.

Some further explorations might include building more complex molecules that also have basic close-to-tetrahedral structures. Since these are plastic models of quantum-mechanics-driven phenomena, be cautious about extrapolating too far from the shapes we have given you. However, if you follow our process and think about what you are trying to model, you can get some deep insights from just trying to get these little models to work.

Summary

This chapter describes some of the chemistry and structure of crystals like ice and diamond. We developed 3D-printed models of the carbon atom itself and then its place in a diamond. We created water molecules and used them to build lattices for two kinds of ice. Finally, we gave you some ideas about how to use these as a teacher and as a basis for 3D-printed science fair projects.

CHAPTER 8

■ ■ ■

Trusses

This, our final chapter in this book, explores simple structures that make up a lot of the infrastructure around us. A *truss* is a structural element that uses the strength of a triangular structure to carry loads with relatively little structural material. Trusses are used just about everywhere that a heavy load has to be carried—bridges, roof supports, and the like.

Planar trusses are thought of as existing in two dimensions (ignoring the thickness of the components), but a *space truss* carries load in three dimesions. This chapter shows you how to create a model of a planar truss. We have also included a model of a simple *tensegrity* structure. These structures are a special type of 3D truss, constructed from a mix of stiff and flexible elements, often with pretty cool-looking results.

There are a lot of computer-aided design (CAD) programs around that can help you figure out the forces accurately if you build a truss in CAD. However, we think that it is also important to build a bit of engineering intuition with models. At the end of the chapter, we talk about some complementary ways to simulate some of these ideas. The models in this chapter are not intended to be used to calculate loading, but rather to build your intuition about how the design of a truss allows it to handle different loads.

Engineering Background

You might first think of bridges when you hear the word *truss*. However, some bridges, like the Henley Street Bridge in Knoxville, Tennessee (see the foreground of Figure 8-1), have been designed with structural members that are arches or boxes. The bridge in the distance (the Gay Street Bridge completed in 1898), however, has a mostly-triangular, 2D truss structure.

Trusses are usually defined as structures made up of thin members that are connected at joints in such a way that force is only applied to any member directly down its axis. That is, any given member is only in compression or tension, and is not resisting any rotation around the joint. An ideal truss is, in fact, built with members connected by pin joints that are free to rotate within a plane.

Figure 8-1. *Two bridges in Knoxville, Tennessee*

In practice, trusses may not have their joints actually free to move. However, the overall structure may be designed so that very little rotational force should ever be applied to the joints, so that in practice it amounts to the same thing. In cases like this, joints are covered with a gusset plate or other reinforcement rather than pin joints that can freely rotate.

Why Triangular Structures?

Trusses have been around in some form since people first made primitive bridges and houses. A triangle is the simplest structure that does not deform easily when a force is applied to one side. Consider the red box on the top of Figure 8-2 and imagine that its four joints are held together with pins that allow the members to rotate around the pin. If you apply a force to the top of it, it will eventually squash to one side or the other.

However, if there is a triangular cross-brace across the rectangular structure (as shown in the blue diagram) the structure is held rigid and cannot collapse without changing the length of at least one of the members. In order for the blue rectangle to collapse like the red one, the cross-brace would have to get longer. This cross-member is then experiencing tensile force. Collapsing the opposite direction would instead apply a compressive force, because it would have to get shorter to allow a collapse. This is true even if the members are free to rotate around the joints holding them together.

158

Simplified analysis of trusses like these assumes the structure is two-dimensional, that its weight is negligable compared to the load it is supporting, and that all forces are applied along the axis of thin members in the 2D plane of the truss. If that is the case, you can figure out the force on each member by adding up the forces in two dimensions in each joint. This type of analysis also has to allow for the fact that some joints will be experiencing some sort of external force (at the ends of a bridge, for example).

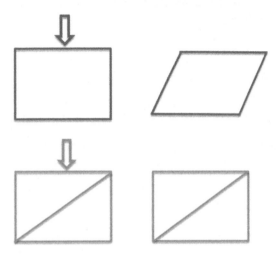

Figure 8-2. *Forces in rectangular and triangular cross-section structures*

Forces on Planar ("2D") Truss Members

When you add up the loads on each member, you wind up with several equations to balance the forces at each of the joints. Sometimes you can solve these sets of simple equations and get a useful result. (Other times you may have to make some assumptions or use more sophisticated techniques.) More complex analysis allowing for the reality of 3D forces, materials properties, and so on these days is usually done with specialized software.

Under static loads, some members of a truss will be in tension (being pulled on each end) and others in compression (being pushed in along its length, as you would if you held a bar between your palms and pushed your palms inward). Some materials are stronger in tension or in compression, so if you know ahead of time what type of force that particular bar will have to take, you can design more efficiently.

■ **Note** We do not get into how to calculate these loads here, since the subject is complex and more appropriate for follow-on projects. A first look at the issues for the 2D problem is described well at https://en.wikipedia.org/wiki/Truss, and you can find more resources by searching on *free body diagram truss bridge*. R.C. Hibbler's *Structural Analysis*, 4th Edition (Prentice Hall, 1999) is a good undergraduate structures textbook if you want to step up to the college-level version of this analysis.

The Space (3D) Truss

The 2D model of a planar truss applies if the loading applied to the truss is all in one plane. But suppose you want to hold up a more complex 3D load? A *space* (or 3D) truss will be needed, sometimes called a *space frame*.

These structures are often used on the back of billboards, as the underside of shade canopies, and other places that a large, often-flat object needs to be held up somehow without using heavy structures or too many supports in the middle of the span. A frame like this has hundreds or thousands of joints, so it becomes impractical to analyze them by writing equations for every joint. More complex methods and software are usually needed to analyze a space frame.

There are a lot of ways to make a simple space-filling truss with various construction toys, or marshmallows and uncooked spaghetti, or any number of other everyday objects. We do not think 3D printing will add a lot to that experience, so instead we are going to show you how to create a somewhat more exotic space-filling structure using *tensegrity*.

Tensegrity Structures

Tensegrity structures use stiff members connected by strings or light cables (https://en.wikipedia.org/wiki/Tensegrity). They are designed so that the cables are always in tension, while the stiff members are always in compression. Buckminster Fuller and artist Ken Snelson popularized the concept. Fuller patented a lot of key aspects of their architectural use in the 1960s through 1980s.

If you are interested in these structures and related ones like those in Fuller's work, you may find some good material for some interesting projects by building on our simple start here. Biologists find tensegrity structures interesting too, because bones and tendons are this type of structure. We will have a bit more about this in the later section "Where to Learn More."

The Models

In this chapter, we give you a few models to play with to build some intuition. There are a lot of other good ways to play with trusses (see "Where to Learn More"), and what we tried to do in this chapter was to create a few unique models that take advantage of 3D printing's strengths.

2D Truss Model

Creating a 2D truss model is a little subtler than it seems. For a 2D truss model to be reasonably accurate, the joints between members need to be pin joints—that is, they need to rotate freely and not move into the third dimension when forces are applied. However, pin joints are pretty difficult to do well with a consumer 3D printer (due to overhang issues and the relative weakness of inter-layer bonds), particularly in a general model that allows the user to create relatively arbitrary trusses.

We decided that a student could functionally model a truss in any number of ways. However, most of these "toy trusses" are fragile and hard to play with too assertively. The model in Listing 8-1 and Figure 8-3 may look a little strange at first glance. However, it allows you to hold the ends (as shown in Figure 8-3) and to see where members compress and expand (under a downward loading in the center, for example).

■ **Note**　Since the "spring" members introduce some effects of their own, the joints are not perfect pin joints. However, we feel it gives some interesting qualitative insights. The compression and expansion under load is a little hard to see in Figure 8-3, but is more apparent when you load and unload the truss dynamically.

Listing 8-1. The 2D Truss

```
// OpenSCAD model to print out a 2D truss
// File name: 2DTruss.scad
// Program creates a 2D truss with members made of simulated springs

beam_width = 3;    // thickness of the truss members, mm
beam_length = 50;  // Max length of the truss,mm
spring_width = 15; // Width of the spring
spring_thick = 1;  // How thick (in the x-y plane) the members in the turn
                   // of the spring arc, mm
spring_gap = 3.3;  // Gap between turns of the spring
spring_turns = 9;  // number of turns in the springy part of each member
spring_pos = (spring_width + spring_thick + spring_gap) * 2/3;
plane_thick = 20;  // depth of the truss in the "third dimension"

triangles = 5; //number of triangles in the truss (should be an odd number)

$fs = .5;
$fa = 2;

// Take the 2D truss and extrude it for plane_thick mm to create the third
// dimension
linear_extrude(plane_thick) {
  for(i = [0:triangles - 1])
```

```
      translate([i * beam_length / 2, (i % 2) * beam_length * sqrt(3)/2, 0])
        beam();
    for(i = [0:triangles])
      translate([i * beam_length / 2, (i % 2) * beam_length * sqrt(3)/2, 0])
        rotate(60 * ((i % 2) ? -1 : 1))
          beam();
}

//Create the truss members with the "spring" inserted in mid-member
module beam(l = beam_length, w = beam_width) {
  spring(l / 2 - (spring_gap + spring_thick) * (spring_turns + 1) / 2)
    offset(w/2) square([l, .01]);
  for(i = [0, 1]) translate([i * beam_length, 0, 0]) circle(beam_width * 1.5);
}

//create the springs in each member by wrapping a curve around a set spacing
module spring(p = 0, w = spring_width, t = spring_thick, g = spring_gap,
s = spring_turns) {
  difference() {
    union() {
      if($children) for(i = [0: $children - 1]) children(i);
      for(i = [0:s]) translate([(i + .5) * (g + t) + p, 0, 0])
      mirror([0, i % 2, 0])
        difference() {
          translate([-.005, 0, 0]) offset(g/2 + t)
            square([.01, (w/2 - g/2 - t) * sin((i + .5)/(s + 1) * 180)]);
          translate([0, -g - t, 0])
            square((g + t) * 2, center = true);
        }
    }
    for(i = [0:s]) mirror([0, i % 2, 0]) translate([(i + .5) * (g + t) +
    p, 0, 0]) {
      translate([0, -w, 0]) offset(g/2)
        square([.01, (w/2 - g/2 - t) * sin((i + .5)/(s + 1) * 180) * 2 +
        w * 2], center = true);
      difference() {
        translate([0, -g - t, 0])
          square((g + t) * 2, center = true);
        for(j = [1, -1]) mirror([0, 1, 0]) translate([j * (g + t), -w, 0])
        offset(g/2 + t)
          square([.01, w - g - t * 2 + w * 2], center = true);
      }
    }
  }
}
```

162

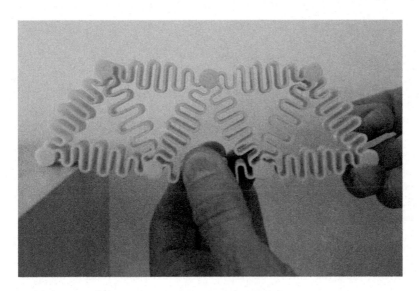

Figure 8-3. *The springy-member 2D truss simulator*

■ **Caution**   Remember that this is a 2D truss, so resist the temptation to twist the model out of the plane. The "springs" are stiff in that direction to try and make it as close to 2D behavior as possible.

We encourage you to create a couple or three of these 2D trusses and play around with different support and loading scenarios. These are designed to be printed flat (with the layers parallel to the truss's plane) which will keep any layer-boundary effects or delaminations from affecting the 2D behavior. These might be good "pass-around" handouts to have in a class that is preparing to build trusses with construction toys or other materials.

Figure 8-4 shows the same model as in Figure 8-3, but now supported all along the bottom and with one pressure point. Although there are a lot of distortions (notably that the endpoints on the bottom were not held in place), it is still clear to see how the triangular structure prevents the area right under that load from collapsing. You can also see how some of the members are in tension while others compress.

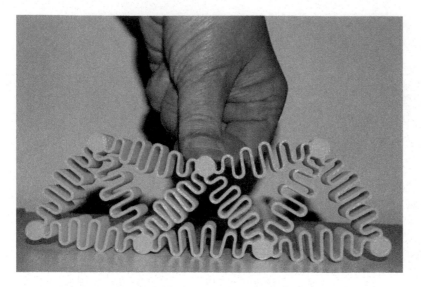

Figure 8-4. *Loading from above*

The model in Listing 8-1 has a variety of parameters that allow you to vary how much of each member is made springy and the relative sizes of the members and features (as well as how many triangles you can have). You may want to vary these and see what combination gets you closest to simulating the idealized truss with its pin joints and stiff members.

Tensegrity Structure Model

Next, we look at creating a demonstration of tensegrity—a way to use stiff members (like those in the trusses we just talked about) in combination with flexible members like cables, string, or rubber bands. The model in Listing 8-2 creates a single element. You should print three of them for the simple prism structure, and six to make an icosahedron (20-sided polyhedron). You also will need three *identical* rubber bands for the prism, and six for the icosahedron.

In general, you can find an optimum length for the cross-bracing strings (here, rubber bands) either by experimenting until you get things tight, or by diving into the mathematics of these structures (www.tensegriteit.nl/e-simple.html). The rubber bands are the most forgiving way we found to build the structure.

In the section "Learning Like a Maker," we discuss how much iteration was needed to come up with this. In the next section, we talk you through assembling the 3-rod tensegrity prism (Figure 8-5) and, in the section after that, the general way you would extend it for the octahedron (Figure 8-6).

Listing 8-2. Tensegrity Truss Members

```
//Program to print tensegrity beam
//File name: tensegrityBeam.scad

l = 120;    // length of the rod
w = 6;      // width of the rod, mm
h = 3;      // depth in third dimension
hole = .5;  // parameter to round off the edges of the slot

$fs = .5;
$fa = 2;

difference() {
  linear_extrude(h, convexity = 5) offset((w - hole) * .24)
  offset((w - hole) * -.24) difference() {
    square([w, l], center = true);
    for(i = [1, -1]) translate([0, i * l / 2, 0]) square([hole, w * 2],
    center = true);
  }
  for(i = [1, -1], j = [0, 1]) {
    translate([0, 0, h / 2]) mirror([0, 0, j]) translate([0, i * l / 2,
    -h / 2 - 1]) hull() {
      linear_extrude(1 + hole) offset(-hole/2 + .1) square([hole, w * 2],
      center = true);
      linear_extrude(1) offset(hole/2 + .1) square([hole, w * 2],
      center = true);
    }
  }
}
```

Figure 8-5. *The 3-rod tensegrity prism*

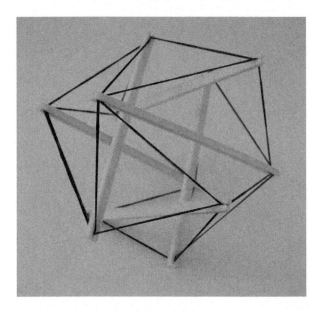

Figure 8-6. *The 6-rod tensegrity icosahedron*

Assembling the 3-Rod Tensegrity Prism

The tensegrity structures are a little tricky to assemble. We take you step by step through assembling a 3-member tensegrity prism. Print three of the members generated by the model in Listing 8-2 and label them, as shown in Figure 8-7.

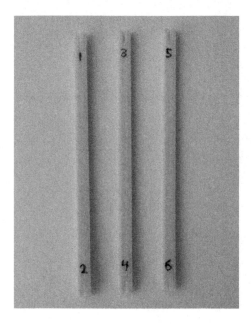

Figure 8-7. *The labeled tensegrity rods*

■ **Tip** We labeled the rods in our test prism with numbers—odd number on top, even number on bottom. Thus we have rod 1-2, rod 3-4, and rod 5-6. You can see them in Figure 8-7. We refer to the rods by these numbers in what follows. Rod 1-2 is just *one* rod, not two—with end 1 and end 2.

Now put a rubber band over each of the rods, through the slit and over front and back (Figure 8-8). Check that the tension front and back is the same, and that the rubber bands on all three rods are exterting about the same tension as each other (Figure 8-9). Otherwise, the structure may be hard to put together. You may need to test out a few rubber bands to get three that are the same as each other.

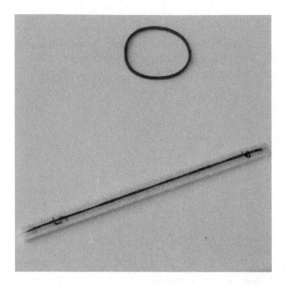

Figure 8-8. *A rod with rubber band (and the unstretched band, for scale)*

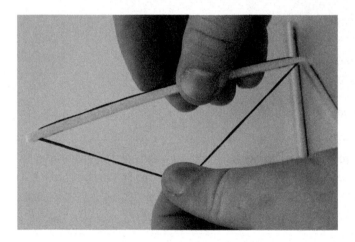

Figure 8-9. *Testing the tension on the rubber band before starting to assemble*

■ **Tip** Keep the odd-numbered ends up and pointing away from you. Pull on rubber bands in the middle of their open space, as in Figure 8-9.

To start assembling, pick up rods 1-2 and 3-4. Pull up the band on 1-2 and hook the middle of rod 1-2's "front" band onto end 3 of rod 3-4 (Figure 8-10).

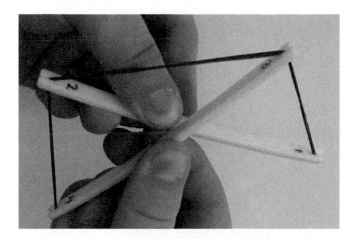

Figure 8-10. *Hooking the first two pieces together*

Next cross rod 3-4 over rod 1-2 so that the remaining rubber bands are on the "outside" of the crossed plastic bars (Figure 8-11).

Figure 8-11. *Lining up rods 1-2 and 3-4 for the next step. Note that rod 3-4 has a rubber band still stretched across its "front," and rod 1-2 has one across its "back."*

Pick up rod 5-6 and put in the "V" of the space between 1-2 and 3-4. Use the band on one side of rod 5-6 to hook onto end 1 of rod 1-2 and end 4 of rod 3-4 (Figure 8-12).

Figure 8-12. *Adding rod 5-6*

Now take the remaining rubber band on rod 3-4 and hook it on end 5 and take the remaining rubber band on rod 1-2 and hook it on end 6. You are done! Now you may need to fiddle with it a bit by gently removing the rubber bands from the end slits and adjusting where along the length of the rubber band they connect to square things up a bit.

The "top" should be a relatively flat equilateral triangle, as should the bottom. These should have single rubber band strands. The three vertical pieces should all be doubled up (Figure 8-13). You are looking "down" and through the top triangle here, which joins ends 1, 3, and 5. The bottom triangle joins ends 2, 4, and 6. The verticals run between ends 2 and 3, 4 and 5, and 1 and 6.

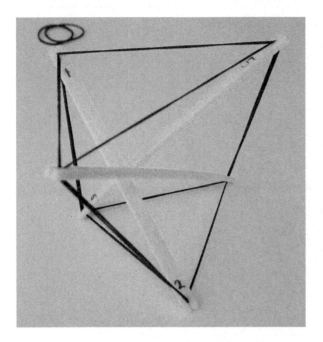

Figure 8-13. *The finished product, looking through the top triangle*

Hints for Assembling an Icosahedron

The icosahedron is a lot tricker. If you decide to assemble one, you may want to ask a friend (or two) to provide extra hands to hold the pieces in place. We do not walk through it step by step here, but we do give you the following hints so you can try it on your own:

- Every link is a single rubber band strand (as opposed to some of them being doubled up, as is the case with the prism).

- While in both cases there are two rubber bands going through each node, rubber bands go off in four directions from each node in the icosahedron, but only in three directions (two of them doubled up together) in the prism.

Figure 8-14 is another view of the iscosahedron.

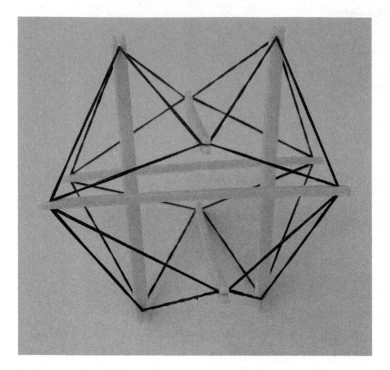

Figure 8-14. *Another view of the isocahedron (compare to Figure 8-6)*

■ **Note**   These trusses are not all that strong as printed, so be cautious if you want to see if you can put something light on top and see if it will stand. Try to avoid very old or previously used rubber bands (which might snap). Be careful not to shoot rubber bands off the ends of a beam during assembly.

Printing These Models

The 2D truss should be printed with a *raft* (a layer of material on the printer platform—see Appendix A). Otherwise, the truss might not have a lot of contact with the printer bed and might be torn off during the printing process. You should not use a brim, as it will affect the compressibility of the spring on one side (so that it will no longer act as a planar truss) if not removed perfectly. Figure 8-15 shows the 2D truss on the print bed with its raft, and Figure 8-16 shows the truss and raft after the two were separated (the truss pulled off the raft and left it behind on the print bed).

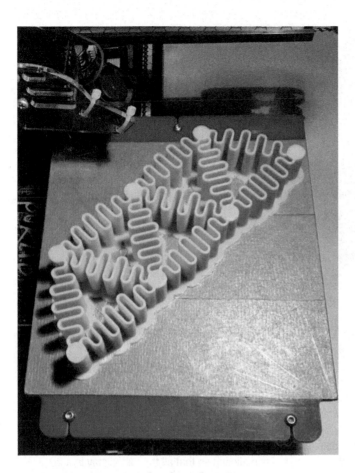

Figure 8-15. *2D truss with raft, on the printer*

The tensegrity elements are very simple to print, except that we recommend that you print them with the thickest layers you can with your printer (a bit smaller than your nozzle diameter is the limiting factor—we printed ours with a 0.4 layer height, on a printer with a 0.5 mm diameter nozzle). In addition to printing faster, printing with thick layers will round off the edges a bit, making them less likely to snap the rubber bands. The beams may warp a bit, which would normally be bad for a truss because it would make the members buckle more easily under compression, but the rubber bands should not exert nearly enough force for this to be a problem. The difficulties in that model lie in the assembly. The key there is to go about it slowly and carefully, and to be sure all your rubber bands are as identical as possible.

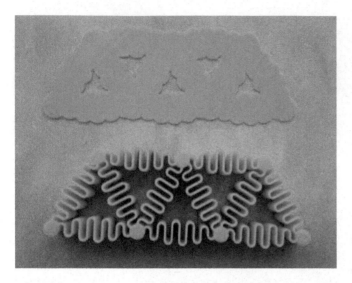

Figure 8-16. *2D truss, separated from the raft (same as in previous figure)*

THINKING ABOUT THE MODELS: LEARNING LIKE A MAKER

As with many of our models, we were surprised by how difficult it was to make even a simple 2D truss that would behave accurately. We went through many iterations (Figure 8-17) of how and where to place the springy part to mimic a pin joint as much as possible. We decided early on we did not want an actual pin joint, since they are difficult to print well and hard to keep aligned so that all the forces stay in a 2D plane. The trusses in Figure 8-17, except for the current one on the lower right, were developed with past iterations of the code for the model, not the one in Listing 8-1.

For the tensegrity models, we had an assortment of failures. Our first model had a hole at the end of each member, rather than a slit at each end. This made it very hard to attach the string. After a lot of fussing with various types of connectors and clips to hold on the bands (Figure 8-18), Rich hit on the version you see earlier in the chapter. The Y-shaped pieces were intended to be temporary scaffolding to hold together the initial triangles in the prism model, but the final design removed the need for that altogether.

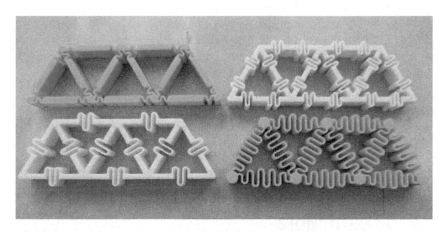

Figure 8-17. *2D truss iterations—moving around the "spring" area, changing its amplitude and how much of each member was "springy"*

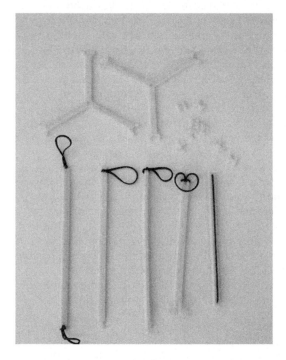

Figure 8-18. *The tensegrity elements and assembly aids that did not work (with the one that did on the bottom right)*

The difficulty we encountered with assembling these structures is actually what convinced us that they were worth including. Removing any member makes a tensegrity become so unstable that it will completely fall apart, which makes it difficult to assemble because it will not be stable until it is finished.

Trying to use string was very frustrating, and we considered using wire for the tensile members so that they would hold their shape, but decided that this was not a true tensegrity. In the end, the way we stretched the rubber bands across the beams allowed the forces to be somewhat balanced, and while the assembly is still a bit tricky, this made it much more manageable.

Where to Learn More

There are various classic kids' engineering contests to build variants of bridges, towers, and trusses. If you have never seen a spaghetti and marshmallow (or toothpick and gumdrop) structure contest, search for it online and see how spectacular the results can be.

There are also a variety of bridge design games online. The group Engineering Encounters runs an annual bridge design contest complete with simulation software, at https://bridgecontest.org. There are also some fun, inexpensive games to allow students to play with creating reasonably realistic 2D trusses to hold up a roadway. Rich is partial to Polybridge (http://store.steampowered.com/app/367450/), and the same store has quite a few other options we have not tried, like the ones resulting from this search: http://store.steampowered.com/search/?term=bridge+construction.

It is interesting (but scary) to read about bridges and other edifices that have failed, but it is a good way of learning about what might go wrong. To read about great failures of bridges, you might read Henry Petroski's boooks, particularly *To Engineer Is Human* (Vintage Books, 1992) and the other books mentioned early in the chapter.

If you want to study a fun example of a moving machine with a lot of space-filling trusses, take a look at Theo Jansen's Strandbeests, (www.strandbeest.com) which he has been "evolving" for years to move efficiently. His leg (truss) design is detailed at www.strandbeest.com/beests_leg.php.

The tensegrity trusses we started you building in this chapter (besides being featured in Buckminster Fuller designs) have appeared in sculptures and in some bridges, notably the Kirulpa Bridge in Brisbane, Australia. Try searching on *tensegrity architecture*. Beyond the man-made, tensegrity structures are of interest in biology, particularly in the mechanics of how bones and tendons work together to create strong structures.

Teacher Tips

Broadly, looking at truss problems can be thought of as fitting into the general middle school or high school "Engineering Design" standards, found at www.nextgenscience.org/topic-arrangement/msengineering-design and www.nextgenscience.org/topic-arrangement/hsengineering-design, respectively.

Alternatively, this material might be used to facilitate discussions of forces and interactions in middle school, although these standards seem to be more about kinematics than the statics issues that we have explored in this chapter: www.nextgenscience.org/topic-arrangement/msforces-and-interactions.

Science Fair Project Ideas

For a relatively simple project, play with some of the parameters for the 2D and 3D truss models. You might see how varying the parameters changes behavior to more closely mimic an ideal pin joint. When you are looking at behavior, we recommend against trying to stress 3D-printed models to failure. The plastic is fairly brittle, and the layer lines may put some stress in places you did not expect. Wear eye protection if you think things may snap.

More complex tensegrity projects are good options for science fair projects, too. How much load can these structures hold? What types of forces are they good at withstanding, and what types of forces are likely to make them collapse? Perhaps you can look into a biological tensegrity structure and figure out how to build something that will mimic the real thing well enough to gain some intuition.

A Few Last Words About Making Things

At the end of this final set of models, we would like to thank you for reading our book and (we hope) actually making things. There are many sophisticated computer programs out there to simulate and calculate answers to many different engineering problems.

But to learn to design something new—and to know when the programs might be outside of their assumptions—you need to develop intuition. We hope that these simple models have served that purpose for you. In some cases (most particularly these last ones), you may learn more by thinking about how these models do *not* fit reality and/or the common idealized models. But how could you make them better? Are the ways these little models work different from reality in a way that teaches you something else?

We hope that if nothing else, we have imparted a reflex to say, in the face of big unknowns, "I don't know, but let's see if we can build a few simple models to find out."

Summary

This chapter developed models of trusses, structures that carry loads by strategically using triangular arrangements of members. The chapter showed you how to print a 2D truss and the elements of a tensegrity truss. We also looked at applications of trusses and ideas for more explorations.

APPENDIX A

■ ■ ■

3D Printing

This book assumes that you know a little about 3D printing already. However, if not, this appendix will get you started and give you resources to figure things out from here.

The 3D Printing Process

First, we should say that you do not just "hit print." The amount of expertise and knowledge required is probably more analogous to cooking, or perhaps to using a sewing machine. 3D printing is rapidly evolving, too, so the details of what we say here may change, although we expect the basic ideas to stay the same for a while.

Having said all that, 3D printing requires three steps. Figure A-1 shows you the overall workflow for creating something with a 3D printer. In this appendix, we concentrate on two free progams that together cover the three parts of creating a 3D print: making a 3D model (in this case, with OpenSCAD), *slicing* that model into layers, and loading the sliced model onto a printer (with MatterControl for those latter two steps).

Figure A-1. *3D-printing workflow with OpenSCAD and MatterControl*

Filament-based 3D Printing

3D prints are created by melting plastic filament and then laying up that melted filament a layer at a time. Layers are very thin—typically 0.2 mm or so. Some types of printers use powder or liquid resins instead of filament. However, the models in this book are intended to be as easy as possible to print on 3D printers that use filament, like the one in Figure A-2 (a Deezmaker Bukito).

Figure A-2. *A filament spool and 3D printer*

The spool of white material next to the printer is PLA (polylactic acid) filament, like that used for the prints in this book. PLA is a corn-based, biodegradable plastic that is one of the commonest materials for 3D-printing filament. Other common filament plastics, like ABS, should work fine as well, but we only tested the prints in PLA. Filament is typically sold on spools of 1 kg or 1 lb of material. The one in Figure A-2 is a 1 kg spool.

File Types

The three steps required to create a 3D print correspond to three different types of file on your computer. In the case of the OpenSCAD 3D models in this book, the models are stored in files that end in .scad. When you are done working on the model in OpenSCAD, you save the final version in a .scad file and also *export* the file to one in the .stl format. The .stl format is a de facto standard for consumer 3D-printable models. Some vintages of Windows do not like the .stl suffix and think it is some sort of security file, but just ignore that and load the file into your slicing program.

For the next steps, MatterControl (or your printer's equivalent software) takes in an .stl file and outputs a .gcode file. The .gcode format (or an equivalent format, such as a .x3g file) is what actually runs on your printer. If your printer uses proprietary software, that software may or may not reveal this file to the user.

Next will walk through OpenSCAD and MatterControl in turn and give you pointers on getting started with each one.

■ **Tip** If you want more detail about 3D printing (including some discussion of post-processing your print or using 3D prints in the sand-casting process), you might consider Joan's book *Mastering 3D Printing* (Apress, 2014). If you want to focus on using the MatterControl software in particular and want more of a detailed user guide, you can instead get Joan and Rich's *3D Printing with MatterControl* (Apress, 2015). Both books review how to get started in 3D printing. See the "MatterControl" section of this appendix to see how to tell whether MatterControl supports your 3D printer. If not, your 3D printer probably came with an equivalent proprietary program.

OpenSCAD

The OpenSCAD program allows you to develop models in a style that sort of looks like the C/Java/Python family of programming languages. It is free and open source, and we want to acknowledge and thank Marius Kintel and the many other contributors and maintainers of the program. You can look at any of the models in this book to see the syntax.

Downloading OpenSCAD

You can download OpenSCAD from www.openscad.org, and an excellent user manual is available at www.openscad.org/documentation.html. Download OpenSCAD and install it per the instructions on the download site. OpenSCAD is available in versions for Linux/UNIX, Windows, and Mac OS X. The models in this book were tested with version 2015.03-3 for Mac OS X. If you are a longtime OpenSCAD user and have an older version than that, you may need to update to the current version to be able to run the models in this book, which take advantage of some recently added features.

Editing the Models

Briefly, to edit one of the models in this book, you would proceed as follows. First you would obtain the relevant .scad file for the model you are interested in. (See the "Repositories" note at the end of this appendix.)

Once you have the file and OpenSCAD is open, click File ➤ Open and open the .scad file. If you do not see the model listing, go to View and uncheck Hide Editor so you can see it. Now, make any changes you feel you need to make and click Design ➤ Preview to see if you have created what you intended. Repeat until you think you are done.

■ **Tip** In OpenSCAD, Design ➤ Preview creates an object you can view but cannot export. It is a lot faster than a full render, which can take a long time for some of the models in this book. Use this to preview models as you are making changes.

When you have your final model, go to Design ➤ Render to create a model that can be exported for 3D printing. Once you have compiled a file, you can export an .stl file by clicking File ➤ Export ➤ Export as STL. Figure A-3 is a screen shot of OpenSCAD with the flower from Chapter 6.

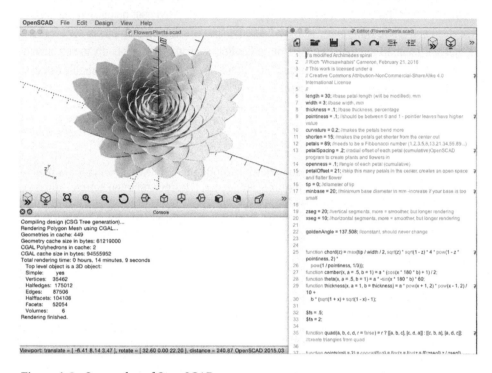

Figure A-3. *Screen shot of OpenSCAD*

Ideosyncracies of OpenSCAD

If you are a programmer, OpenSCAD can be a little disconcerting because its syntax looks like that of the C/Java/Python family of languages. But it is not a full programming language and has a few ideosyncracies. The biggest one is that OpenSCAD does not have true variables, as one would define them in other programming languages. The variables in our models are best thought of as constants. You can assign another value to a variable, but (as would be true in algebra) $y = y + 1$ is *not* a valid statement in OpenSCAD. See the manual section on variables for details and examples at `https://en.wikibooks.org/wiki/OpenSCAD_User_Manual/General#Variables`.

Functions in OpenSCAD are also functions in the mathematical sense. They return a value, but cannot perform other tasks beyond a single mathematical formula along the way. OpenSCAD has *modules* that are closer to what an experienced programmer will expect from a function.

182

MatterControl

Once you have exported your .stl file from OpenSCAD, you need to run a program that can convert the model into commands to drive your 3D printer. This section describes MatterControl, a free and open source program supported by our friends at MatterHackers. MatterControl is compatible with many types of 3D printer, though some proprietary ones do not use the same standard as others.

Printers MatterControl Supports

The list of printer models that MatterControl supports is at `www.mattercontrol.com/#jumpSupportedModels`. (If your printer is not listed there, MatterControl does not include settings for it, but you should be able to configure MatterControl to work with any printer that uses .gcode files). If your printer is not supported by MatterControl, your manufacturer likely has created a proprietary program that will also take an .stl file as its input. Check your manufacturer's documentation, or contact MatterHackers to see if an existing 3D-printer profile can be used for your machine.

Downloading and Installing MatterControl

Assuming that your printer is supported, you can download MatterControl at `mattercontrol.com`, in versions for Mac OS X, Windows, and Linux. There is some documentation linked to the download page (as of this writing, through a link entitled Learn More).

Using MatterControl

MatterControl is a very capable and complex program. To take full advantage, you can use its online documentation or get a copy of our book on MatterControl that we noted earlier. This section is just a very quick guide to getting started.

First you will need to tell MatterControl what type of 3D printer you have. On the home screen, you can use the File ➤ Add A Printer item and its subsequent dialogs to set up your printer. Some printers need to be actively connected to a computer, and some can run off an SD card or wireless connection. See MatterHackers' documentation and your manufacturer's suggestions for this step.

Once you have your printer squared away, you will need to load in an .stl file. You can either use the +Add button, shown on the lower left of Figure A-1, or the menu by clicking File ➤ Add File to Queue (which imports an .stl file to be printed), as shown in Figure A-4.

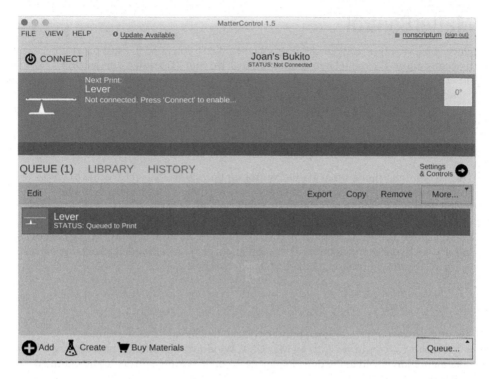

Figure A-4. *The MatterControl home screen*

If you mouse over an item in the queue (the lever from Chapter 5, in this case), you will see two options, View and Remove, as shown in Figure A-5. Remove removes the file from the queue (deletes it from MatterControl's queue). View starts the process of preparing the file to print.

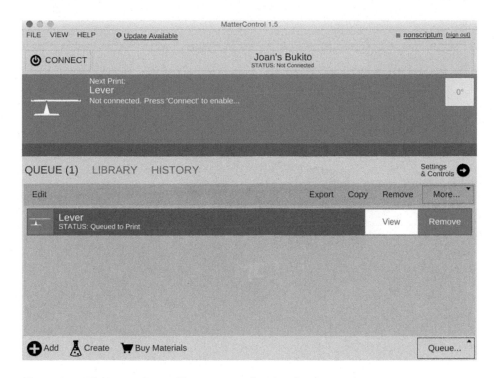

Figure A-5. *The MatterControl home screen showing the View option*

After you click View, you will see a screen like that in Figure A-6. The screen that comes up (3D VIEW) shows your print as it will lie on your 3D printer's print bed. If it is hanging off the ends or otherwise problematic, there are tools you can use (after clicking Edit) to rectify the problems. When you are done, be sure to click Save to save your changes before the final creation of your printable file.

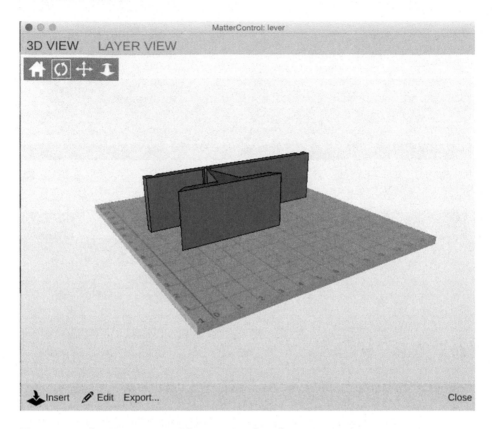

Figure A-6. The View screen, with 3D VIEW selected

Once you are done editing and are satisfied that the file is ready to 3D print, select LAYER VIEW. The program will ask you to click Generate if you have not generated your printable file yet. This step breaks the model into layers that can be printed and creates the commands that will move around the print head and push filament where it needs to be. You can see the LAYER VIEW screen in Figure A-7. The LAYER VIEW screen also tells you how long the print will take, more or less, and how much filament (3D-printing raw material) it will use up.

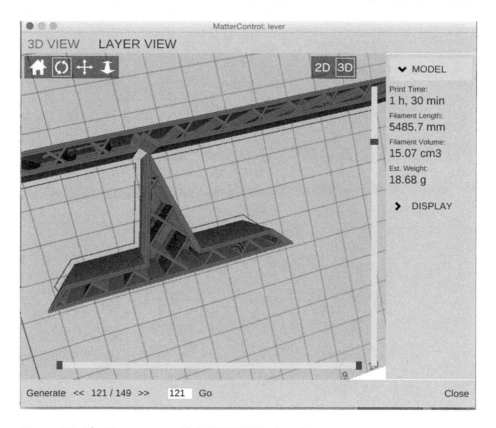

Figure A-7. The View screen, with LAYER VIEW selected

If this looks good, go back to the home screen (Figure A-4) and click Export (in the middle of the screen). Then select Export as Gcode. If your printer needs to be actively connected to a computer, at this point you could send the file to the printer.

Settings

Hypothetically, the discussion thus far should just work as stated, and you will have gone from a model in this book to a physical one in your hand. Real life with a 3D printer is not always that simple, though. 3D printers have a lot of different settings, because tweaking is needed sometimes. If you click the Settings&Controls button on the home screen (Figure A-4), you will find yourself at a page like the one in Figure A-8.

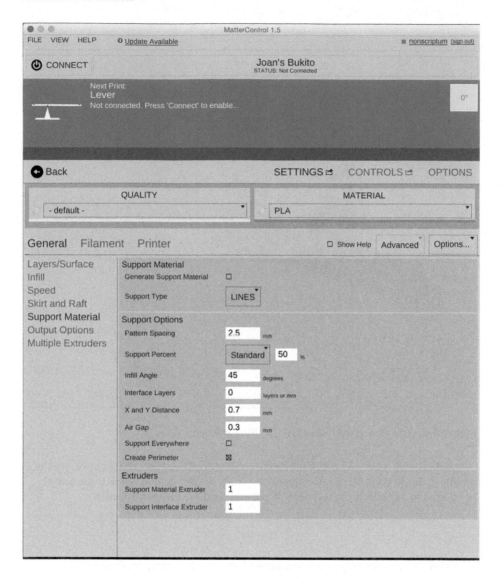

Figure A-8. *The Settings&Controls screen*

In Figure A-8 you see SETTINGS, CONTROLS, and OPTIONS. Probably as a beginner you will not touch anything in OPTIONS except for perhaps selecting MatterSlice as your Slice Engine, if it has not already defaulted there. CONTROLS are functions you will use to interact with your printer to solve a problem or set up your printer, which we will not explore here.

That leaves SETTINGS. The models in this book were, for the most part, designed to be as simple to print as possible. That means you should be able to get away with pretty generic settings. This section covers some that you might need to change, particularly General ➤ Support Material and General ➤ Skirt and Raft.

Support

Since a filament-based 3D printer builds up prints from a platform, if a piece sticks out sideways higher up on a print, that part will just fall down if support material is not built ahead of time to support it. Most of the models in this book have been designed to avoid support. Some of the botanical models in Chapter 6 might require it, depending on your settings. You can look in the LAYER VIEW to see if it looks like the overhangs will be too large to manage without support.

There is a rule of thumb that a slope can overhang by about 45 degrees before support is necessary. However, sometimes you can push your luck. Figures A-9 through A-11 are the flower on the cover of this book (the model is in Chapter 6). It was printed without support. You can see that it overhangs pretty significantly, but we suspected the organic shape would survive without support. You can see a little raggedness on the farthest-out petals, particularly in the view from below. On the bottom, plastic would have been deposited partially in air without support, which is why it is particularly rough there.

Figure A-9. *The flower from Chapter 6 from above*

Figure A-10. *The flower from Chapter 6 from the side to show the extent of unsupported overhangs*

Figure A-11. *The flower from Chapter 6 from below*

If you do need to add support, check the Generate Support Material box under General ➤ Support Material. In general, the less support you have to generate (and then pick off), the better. If you have something really complex, you may have to check the Support Everywhere box. This creates support as needed, including in nooks and crannies of the model where it may be hard to remove. Be sure to preview your model in LAYER VIEW first to see how it looks.

Figure A-12 shows what the same flower model looks like with support everywhere plus a raft. You can see why you might try to avoid it, both in terms of using filament and also in print time. Figure A-13 shows the completed print with the support still attached.

You can see that it will be difficult to pick off the support that landed between petals, or under the thinner parts of the outer petals. Figure A-2 was taken while the printer was partway through this print. You can see all the support around the periphery of the print.

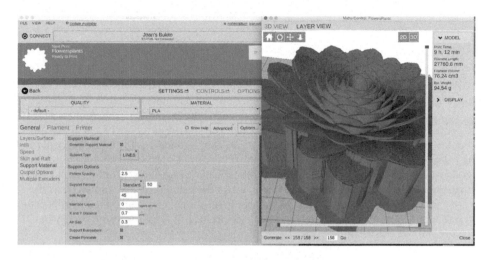

Figure A-12. *MatterControl screen shot of the same print with Support Everywhere*

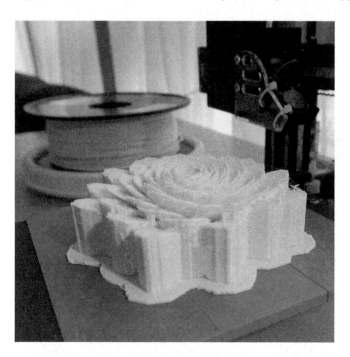

Figure A-13. *The completed flower-with-support print, with the support still on it*

■ **Note**   MatterControl will not show support in the 3D VIEW. It does not generate the support until layers are generated for the LAYER VIEW.

Raft

Some of the models in this book depend on your printer's bed being pretty smooth and flat so that multiple pieces can be printed and then arranged flush with each other (like the airplane wing with the sting in Chapter 4, or the water molecule halves in Chapter 7).

If your printer's bed is not very flat, you can print these parts on a raft. A *raft* is a thin layer that prints first on the platform, and then the model prints on top of it. If things are not fitting together well, adding a raft (General ➤ Skirt and Raft) is an option. You will need to remove the raft, though, which may be difficult to do cleanly if your raft settings have not been tuned to allow it to release from the print. You may want to test it with a smaller piece to make sure the raft will peel away in one piece before printing a larger model on a raft.

Figure A-14 shows the same item we have been showing through the appendix with a raft added. Note that you would not use a raft for this print—this is just to show what changes if you add a raft.

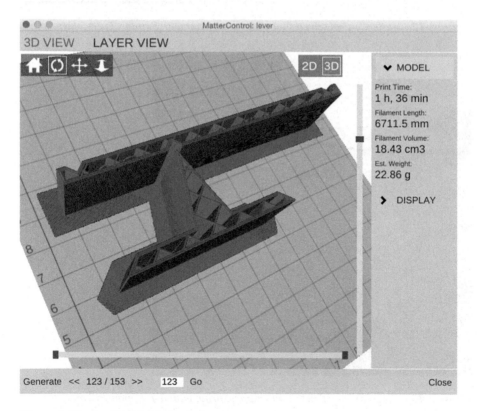

Figure A-14.   A raft added to the lever

You will notice in the same grouping of settings some choices referring to a skirt. A *skirt* is a line drawn around the model's first layer to prime the nozzle. If you make a skirt attached (or 0 mm away from the model), it is usually called a *brim* (as in hat brim). A brim can help hold prints onto the print bed, though it will not help flatten the bottom of a print the way a raft will.

■ **Caution**   If you change a setting, be sure to click SAVE in the SETTINGS window before going back to the LAYER VIEW window and generating a new printable file. Otherwise, it is easy to accidentally revert any unsaved settings.

Other Considerations for These Models

For the most part, these models were printed in PLA with a layer height of 0.2 mm (General ➤ Layers/Surface) with 15% infill (General ➤ Infill). Your printer defaults may be different than this, and you may want to do a few tests with one of our simpler prints (like the lever from Chapter 4) to establish your favorite basic settings.

Archives and Repositories

There is a link for the source for the OpenSCAD models on this book's copyright page. The files archived there are the ones shown in the book. In addition, we have a repository which may have more current versions at https://github.com/whosawhatsis/ 3DP-Science-Projects.

If you develop any new models around these, we hope you will add them to the open source repositories and help build out a community of scientific learners.

Links

This Appendix aggregates all the links in the book in one place for convenient reference. If a link appeared in more than one chapter, it is listed here under the chapter in which it first appeared.

About the Authors

Nonscriptum LLC: www.nonscriptum.com

Chapter 1: 3D Math Functions

OpenSCAD 3D modeling software: www.openscad.org

MatterControl printer control software: www.mattercontrol.com

Creative Commons licenses: http://creativecommons.org/licenses/by-nc-sa/4.0/

OpenSCAD manual: https://en.wikibooks.org/wiki/OpenSCAD_User_Manual/Mathematical_Functions

Python computer language documentation: https://docs.python.org/2/index.html

The Khan Academy online learning: www.khanacademy.org

Elizabeth Denne's math modeling sites:

http://mathvis.academic.wlu.edu/
http://home.wlu.edu/~dennee/math_vis.html
http://www.thingiverse.com/dennedesigns/about

Mathematical sculptor Bathsheba Grossman: www.bathsheba.com

Mathematical sculptor Henry Segerman: www.shapeways.com/shops/henryseg

Paul Nylander math models: http://bugman123.com/

Miscellaneous Math models online:

www.thingiverse.com/explore/newest/learning/math
www.youmagine.com

Chapter 2: Light and Other Waves

principle of superposition: https://en.wikipedia.org/wiki/Superposition_principle

diffraction: https://en.wikipedia.org/wiki/Diffraction

Thomas Young double-slit experiment: https://en.wikipedia.org/wiki/Young's_interference_experiment

Khan Academy light waves tutorials: www.khanacademy.org/science/physics/light-waves

Fourier Transforms: https://en.wikipedia.org/wiki/Fourier_transform

Very Large Array radio telescope: www.vla.nrao.edu

Next Generation Science standards: www.nextgenscience.org

Next Generation Science standards related to waves:

www.nextgenscience.org/msps-wer-waves-electromagnetic-radiation
www.nextgenscience.org/4w-waves
www.nextgenscience.org/hs-ps4-3-waves-and-their-applications-technologies-information-transfer
www.nextgenscience.org/4-ps4-1-waves-and-their-applications-technologies-information-transfer

Maxwell's equations: https://en.wikipedia.org/wiki/Maxwell's_equations

Sun's magnetic field: https://en.wikipedia.org/wiki/Heliospheric_current_sheet

Chapter 3: Gravity

Einstein's general relativity: https://en.wikipedia.org/wiki/General_relativity

Gravitational potential: https://en.wikipedia.org/wiki/Gravitational_potential

Gravitational potential well, from cartoon strip XKCD: https://xkcd.com/681/

Gravitational potential well: https://en.wikipedia.org/wiki/Gravity_well

Algol (star system): https://en.wikipedia.org/wiki/Algol

Ellipses: https://en.wikipedia.org/wiki/Ellipse

Kepler's laws: https://en.wikipedia.org/wiki/Kepler's_laws_of_planetary_motion

Newton's Vis Viva equation: https://en.wikipedia.org/wiki/Vis-viva_equation

Halley's comet: https://en.wikipedia.org/wiki/Halley's_Comet

Kepler astronomy space mission: http://kepler.nasa.gov/Mission/discoveries

Next Generation Science Standards applying to gravity etc.:

www.nextgenscience.org/msess-ss-space-systems
www.nextgenscience.org/ms-ess1-2-earths-place-universe

Kepler spacecraft astronomy resources: http://kepler.nasa.gov/education/EducationandPublicOutreachProjects

Algol's brightness: www.skyandtelescope.com/astronomy-blogs/behold-algol-star-secret/

Chapter 4: Airfoils

Kutta condition: www.grc.nasa.gov/www/K-12/airplane/lifteq.html

lift coefficient: (https://en.wikipedia.org/wiki/Lift_coefficient

drag coefficient: https://en.wikipedia.org/wiki/Drag_coefficient

Kutta-Jukowski theorem: https://en.wikipedia.org/wiki/Kutta%E2%80%93Joukowski_theorem

NASA Glenn Beginner's Guide to Aeronautics: www.grc.nasa.gov/www/K-12/airplane/

NACA/NASA history chronology : www.hq.nasa.gov/office/pao/History/Timeline/1930-34.html

The Incomplete Guide to Airfoil Usage: http://m-selig.ae.illinois.edu/ads/aircraft.html

The Incomplete Guide to Airfoil Usage links page: http://m-selig.ae.illinois.edu/ads.html

Wing planforms for kids: www.grc.nasa.gov/www/k-12/airplane/area.html

Wind Tunnel Experiments for Grades 8 - 12: www.grc.nasa.gov/WWW/k-12/airplane/topics.htm

NASA Tech Reports Service http://ntrs.nasa.gov

Site about airfoils in general: http://airfoiltools.com

NASA Glenn Research Center K-12 site: www.grc.nasa.gov/WWW/K-12/airplane/bgt.html

Airplane presentations for teachers: www.grc.nasa.gov/WWW/K-12/airplane/topics.htm

DIY student wind tunnel design: www.sciencebuddies.org/science-fair-projects/wind-tunnel-toc.shtml.

Simpler DIY student wind tunnel design: www.instructables.com/id/DIY-Wind-Tunnel-20-Project-Paperclip/

Science standards about energy and motion: www.nextgenscience.org/msps2-motion-stability-forces-interactions www.nextgenscience.org/msps3-energy

Chapter 5: Simple Machines

Simple machines intro: https://en.wikipedia.org/wiki/Simple_machine

Inclined plane: https://en.wikipedia.org/wiki/Inclined_plane

Screw: https://en.wikipedia.org/wiki/Screw_%28simple_machine%29

Block and tackle: https://en.wikipedia.org/wiki/Block_and_tackle

Museum of Science and Industry in Chicago simple machines page: www.msichicago.org/play/simplemachines/

Edheads simple machines: www.edheads.org/activities/simple-machines/

Rich's Quick Print Gear Bearing: www.youmagine.com/designs/quick-print-gear-bearing

Emmett Lalish gear: www.thingiverse.com/thing:53451

Castilleja School's Bourne Idea Lab: www.castilleja.org/bournidealab

Forces and Interactions science standards: www.nextgenscience.org/msps2-motion-stability-forces-interactions

Energy standards: www.nextgenscience.org/msps3-energy

University of Colorado, Boulder lesson plans: www.teachengineering.org/view_lesson.php?url=collection/cub_/lessons/cub_simp_machines/cub_simp_machines_lesson01.xml

Chapter 6: Plants and Their Ecosystems

Plants: https://en.wikipedia.org/wiki/Plant

Golden ratio: www.mathsisfun.com/numbers/golden-ratio.html

Fibonacci number: https://en.wikipedia.org/wiki/Fibonacci_number

K-2 science standards about interrelationships between plants, animals and environment: www.nextgenscience.org/topic-arrangement/kinterdependent-relationships-ecosystems-animals-plants-and-their-environment

Middle school standards: www.nextgenscience.org/pe/ms-ls2-5-ecosystems-interactions-energy-and-dynamics

High school: www.nextgenscience.org/pe/hs-ls2-7-ecosystems-interactions-energy-and-dynamics

Biology citizen science site: www.inaturalist.org

Chapter 7: Molecules

Periodic table background: https://en.wikipedia.org/wiki/Periodic_table

Royal Chemical Society interactive periodic table: http://www.rsc.org/periodic-table

Schrödinger's Equation: http://en.wikipedia.org/wiki/Schr%C3%B6dinger_equation

Orbitals: https://en.wikipedia.org/wiki/Atomic_orbital

Ice: https://en.wikipedia.org/wiki/Ice

Ice 1c: https://en.wikipedia.org/wiki/Ice_Ic

Hybridization and Hybrid Orbitals: www.khanacademy.org/science/chemistry/chemical-bonds/copy-of-covalent-bonds

Chemwiki: http://chemwiki.ucdavis.edu/Theoretical_Chemistry/Chemical_Bonding/Valence_Bond_Theory

Molecular geometries resulting from different types of bonds: www.kidzsearch.com/wiki/Orbital_hybridization

This video explains hybridization in terms of energy: www.youtube.com/watch?v=HKyobMewXBw

These videos use balloons to model bonding:

www.youtube.com/watch?v=bOKvfvJi-vk
www.youtube.com/watch?v=KbOmxAMHnfE

Water: http://www1.lsbu.ac.uk/water/

Water: www.khanacademy.org/science/biology/water-acids-and-bases/water-as-a-solid-liquid-and-gas/v/liquid-water-denser-than-solid-water-ice

Science standards, chemical reactions: www.nextgenscience.org/topic-arrangement/hschemical-reactions

Matter and its Interactions science standards: www.nextgenscience.org/dci-arrangement/ms-ps1-matter-and-its-interactions

Chapter 8: Trusses

2D truss: https://en.wikipedia.org/wiki/Truss

Tensegrity truss intro: https://en.wikipedia.org/wiki/Tensegrity

Tensegrity in-depth info site: www.tensegriteit.nl/e-simple.html

Bridge contest: https://bridgecontest.org/

Polybridge game site: http://store.steampowered.com/app/367450/

Site to purchase other games: http://store.steampowered.com/search/?term=bridge+construction

Strandbeest main page: www.strandbeest.com

Strandbeest designs page: www.strandbeest.com/beests_leg.php

Engineering Design science standards:

www.nextgenscience.org/topic-arrangement/msengineering-design
www.nextgenscience.org/topic-arrangement/hsengineering-design

Standards for forces and interactions in middle school: www.nextgenscience.org/topic-arrangement/msforces-and-interactions

Appendix A: 3D Printing

Main OpenSCAD documentation page: www.openscad.org/documentation.html

OpenSCAD manual section on variables: https://en.wikibooks.org/wiki/OpenSCAD_User_Manual/General#Variables

MatterControl listing of supported printers: www.mattercontrol.com/#jumpSupportedModels

The author's repository of these models: https://github.com/whosawhatsis/3DP-Science-Projects

Index

CPSIA information can be obtained
at www.ICGtesting.com
Printed in the USA
LVOW02s0314010616
490729LV00008B/143/P